LEARN TO PAINT WITH
OILS

PETER JOHN GARRARD VPRBA, RP, NEAC

COLLINS
GLASGOW & LONDON

INTRODUCTION

To the beginner

This book is designed for those who want to begin to paint in oils. My interest in the beginner goes back a long way to the time when I started to write articles for *The Artist* magazine specifically to help in this direction. It is something that has fascinated me ever since. There have been many how-to-do-it books devoted to teaching beginners and probably the most famous, and in my opinion still one of the best, was *The Elements of Drawing*, written by Ruskin in the nineteenth century. Later, some excellent books were produced in the 1920s.

More recently there have been some series of television programmes which have kindled the desire to paint in many who would not have thought it possible in the past. I do not think any author has been so bold as to say that his book is a substitute for special lessons from your own private artist, and I do not believe a book can take the place of lessons from a good teacher, even when he is working with a group. Writing towards the end of 1979, I know private lessons are unavailable, except for a lucky few, and because of the massive cuts in adult education programmes throughout the UK, classes are fewer and often far away. When I worked on *The Artist* I had countless letters from people overseas who wanted to paint, but for whom the modest provisions of adult education available to some of you were beyond their wildest dreams.

There are two other problems which face the adult beginner. The first is time, because even though we are bombarded with talk about the leisure society and how we are going to fill our spare time, we know we have not as much of it as *they* seem to think. Secondly, when it comes to art many people have an innate modesty, and even more feel diffident because they are starting to learn late in life. This causes them to feel they must not set their sights too high and must learn to draw before they can paint.

I have written this book because I am convinced it is not necessary to learn to draw before you paint, there are ways of learning which can overcome a shortage of time, there are many distinguished artists who have started late in life and because I know that a beginner can paint something which is lovely, and at the same time have a lot of fun doing it. But above all, I have written it because I love painting.

Many people have helped me. There is not space enough to mention them all, but I would like to thank: the many beginners who have taught me a great deal; the kind friends who have made their pictures available and others who have given their thoughts; Michael Petts for his endless patience and excellent photography; John Youé and his editors for all their advice; Royston Davies and George Rowney & Company Limited – without whose materials it would not have been written – and finally, Patricia, Judith, Lucy and Jonathan, without whose help and forbearance it would not have been possible. Have fun and good luck with your painting.

Peter John Garrard

Peter John Garrard

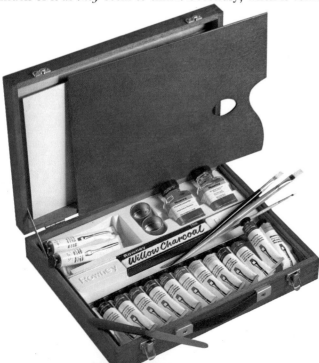

First published 1980
Collins Publishers, Glasgow and London

© Peter John Garrard 1980

Designed and edited by Youé and Spooner Limited
Filmset by Tradespools Limited
Photography by Michael Petts

ISBN 0 00 138301 9

Printed in Great Britain

CONTENTS

PORTRAIT OF AN ARTIST
PETER JOHN GARRARD *VP.RBA, RP, NEAC*

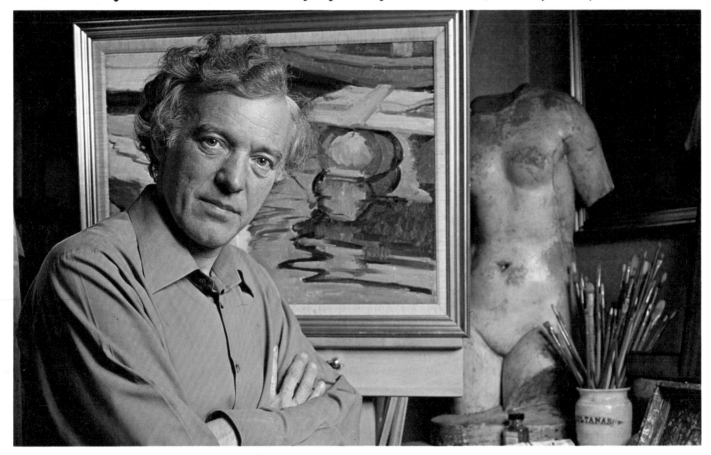

Peter John Garrard was born in Peterborough, Cambridge-shire, and now lives in London with his wife, Patricia, and their three children. A well-known teacher and painter, he is aware of the problems of beginners and has played a part in the development of art education for adults.

His father, Colonel W. V. Garrard, MBE, TD, had always wanted to be a painter, and his interest was passed to his son. After leaving school, Garrard taught Latin and rugger at Summerfields, Oxford, the famous prep school. He gave his first public lecture, on Emily Brönte, at the age of 17, to an undergraduate society at Pembroke College, Oxford. He is particularly proud of this because most of the students were over 30, it being just after the Second World War. While teaching at Summerfields, Garrard studied art at local adult evening classes. He then joined the army, and served with the Suffolk Regiment in Greece during the civil war. When he returned to England, he studied at the Byam Shaw School of Painting and Drawing in London.

While a student he won the Knapping Prize and twice won the David Murray Landscape Scholarship. During his final year at Byam Shaw he was commissioned to paint several landscapes and portraits, and he has since made a name for himself in both teaching and painting. After leaving art school he worked for some time for a firm of restorers and this gave him an abiding interest in the technicalities of paint. Although he does a lot of drawing and watercolour painting, oils have always been Garrard's favourite medium, and he continues to paint mostly realistic portraits and landscapes.

The appeal of Garrard's paintings is international. His work is on display in public and private collections all over the world; in Australia, Canada, France, Germany, Poland, the United States and New Zealand. British public collections boasting his paintings include: the Royal Academy, the Royal Hospital, Chelsea; the Royal Borough of Kensington and Chelsea; Hull City Council, and several hospitals. His works have been sold at numerous art galleries in London and the provinces, in addition to ones in the United States and Switzerland. He has taken part

View from Aigaliers,
63.5 × 76.2cm (25 × 30in)

in three representative exhibitions of British painting over-seas and has held three large one-man exhibitions in London, in 1974, 1976 and 1978. He has had pictures in most of the major mixed exhibitions in London.

He was editor of *The Artist* from 1972 to 1979 and has written articles on painting and drawing for numerous magazines. He was also the author of the ninth edition of *The Artist Guide*, published in 1976.

Garrard's interest in beginners is borne out by his in-volvement in competitions. He was chairman of the Shell and Brooke Bond children's competitions for several years

and has been chairman of the Inveresk Watercolour Painting Competition since its inception. In 1978 and 1979 he was chairman of the judges of the 'Spirit of London' Painting Competition. He is a governor of the Mary Ward Settlement and the Camberwell School of Arts and Crafts, and runs the Mary Ward Centre Art Workshop part-time.

Peter Garrard is the Vice-President of the Royal Society of British Artists and a member of the Royal Society of Portrait Painters, the New English Art Club and the Art Workers Guild. In 1977 he was awarded the de Laszlo Medal by the Royal Society of British Artists.

Virginia and Sophie,
106.7 × 134.6cm
(42 × 53in).
Collection of Jill de Brant

5

'I WOULD LOVE TO PAINT'

In many different ways people say to me: 'I would love to paint but I can't draw a straight line.' Usually there is no time to make more than a polite rejoinder: 'It doesn't matter – just have a go.' However sensible such advice might be, the fact remains that too often people think they must be able to draw before they can start painting. We who teach know that drawing matters, but where we fail so often is that we do not tackle the root of the problem – we start by trying to help the beginner improve his drawing, in other words, we accept his premise.

When first I was a student I learned by drawing plaster casts for many months, then I moved up to life drawing and finally – a great moment – I was allowed to paint a still

life. But before I started the painting, I drew the still life twice; once to work out the design of shapes, then to work out the tone. When my teacher thought I had thoroughly understood these, I was allowed to put brush to canvas. But before I was permitted to put down any colours I had to copy the design onto the canvas and work out the tonal pattern with one paint (Raw Umber). Eventually, I was allowed to put some real colour onto the canvas. As you can imagine, by the time I got to the colour I knew the subject very well, indeed it would be fairer to say too well. The first excitement had gone long ago. Often it was difficult to remember why I had wanted to paint that subject. More important, it was hard to understand what

my teacher meant by 'good drawing' when he insisted this must come first. I was always puzzled: 'Had I drawn well?' I was dependent upon what he meant until I began to understand what he was trying to teach me.

The first thing I want to suggest to you is *start painting immediately*. Do not bother about anything else – have a go. I suggest this not because drawing is unimportant and the way I learned bad, but more because you can learn most satisfactorily what is meant by drawing when you have done some painting. You will find I mention drawing quite often, and try to explain what I mean by it, but I do believe that the best way for you to learn is through painting.

When I try to imagine what you, the reader, are like, my difficulty is that you are everybody. I have known so many people, from all walks of life, who have wanted to paint. There are no special qualifications, the only thing they had in common was a wish to learn, and I suspect, though I have never been able to prove it, that they had all enjoyed making mud pies as small children. But too many of them have a desire to do it the right way and a remembrance of

a childhood teacher telling them drawing must be mastered first. If I can rid you of this at the outset, I will be pleased.

For many people drawing is a great stumbling block because they see it as something at which they ought to excel, but which presents a whole series of difficulties they do not understand. Most people think of drawing as being done with a pencil and as getting the outlines 'correct' and 'filling these in' when they paint. This is so far from the truth that I think it is probably better to start from the other end. Paint first and discover from your own work why drawing is useful – hopefully you will go on to draw (even with a pencil for its own sake) and understand why it can help you.

You may ask what qualifications you require to begin to learn about painting. The only one which matters is a wish to paint and willingness to try. One of the exciting things about painting – why it is different from all other arts – is that even as a humble beginner you can express yourself and the way you paint will be different from anyone else's. All this book can do is to try to help you start on a most worthwhile and absorbing study. Some of you will worry because you are starting to paint late in life – too late to do anything about it. Banish such thoughts from your head – the oldest student I have had is in her late eighties and I know she is getting along very nicely. Some of you will worry that because of other commitments you cannot devote as much time to painting as you would wish, but remember that most professionals would say the same thing. I am very conscious of this need to telescope time and you will find that some of the suggestions I make are designed to make it easier for you to get on, to go a stage further more quickly.

There is one other quality I would commend – patience, particularly patience with me. Remember too that though painting is a serious business, it is something you will enjoy and this enjoyment matters very much.

Don't be afraid to make mistakes – in painting you learn most from correcting them.

OIL PAINTS-WHAT THEY ARE

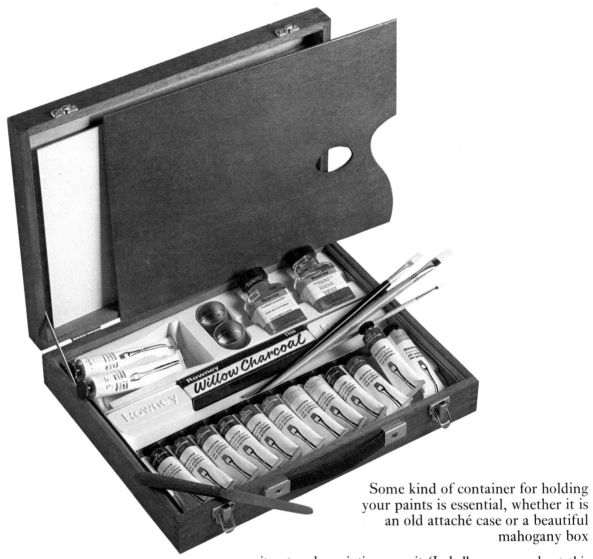

Some kind of container for holding your paints is essential, whether it is an old attaché case or a beautiful mahogany box

Painting with oils is one of the most exciting ways of painting but, to be truthful, for myself at the moment, it is the only way to paint. I like the stuff of oil paint; I enjoy messing about with it; I like the way it can be used thickly and thinly; the way that every touch can be varied, and even the smell pleases me. In short, it is for me the ideal means of expression. I do not mean I do not like to draw, often there are occasions when drawing with a pencil is just what is required, but for sheer personal pleasure I will paint with oils.

As a medium for the beginner it is perfect because it is very easy to correct what you have done either by wiping it out or by painting over it (I shall say more about this later). The great difficulty with other media, such as watercolour, is that correction, when you realize it is necessary, is well nigh impossible. For example, you realize that a colour should be lighter; with oil paint you work over it with the 'right' colour, but with watercolour you can only scrub it down, and this is not easy. Another advantage is that you can place touches of different colours immediately next to each other whilst both are still wet and they will not run into each other. In fact, this is one of the most useful ways of painting, which I will mention often. Oil painting provides you with the greatest range of choices: you can paint rich, dark colours or pale, gentle shades; it lends itself to objective painting, and many abstract painters prefer it above all else. But enough of

Take care of your tubes of paint. The tubes on the left are badly squeezed, which is wasteful. On the right, what you should do

this, by now you should be finding out some of this for yourself because I hope you have started a painting.

There are some disadvantages in using oil paints. For many people, the fact that they do not dry completely for a long while is, I suppose, the most serious (this is discussed on p. 64 in the section on varnishing). I have found slowness of drying a difficulty only when I have been on a painting trip and have to transport home a lot of wet paintings. Again, this can be overcome: if you paint on canvas, place canvas pins at each corner of the canvas and place another canvas on top. Canvas pins hold apart two canvasses, if you have painted on a board, use thin slices of cork and tie the boards together with string.

I imagine that some people would consider the fact that you do have to learn some technical information about the paint a disadvantage. The amount you have to learn can be remarkably small, provided you remember one or two simple rules and do not use too complex a palette of colours. Throughout this book you will find that I mention rules, or rather sensible ways of behaviour. The equipment you need is discussed in the next section and a basic set of colours is described on p. 14.

You may well ask why a beginner should bother about such things. A sensible question, but you will mind if a picture you paint today is in a bad state in two months, if it has cracked all over or the colour has changed. A first basic rule: do not do the drawing or underpainting in Ivory Black because it dries much slower than other colours – if an underneath layer dries more slowly than a top layer it will crack when the top layer dries. From a technical point of view, what you require in the short term will also ensure your paintings last for posterity.

It would help at this point if I described the differences between the media. At their simplest, oil paint is pigment ground in oil; acrylic paint is pigment ground with an acrylic polymer resin; watercolour is pigment mixed with gum arabic and several other ingredients; pure tempera is pigment plus egg yolk (there are variations of this), and tempera emulsion is pigment plus egg and linseed oil. Thus, a paint is composed of pigment plus a vehicle (oil or diluent). For example, you want Yellow Ochre paint: Yellow Ochre ground with linseed oil will make a paint. But this simplification is not true of most paints you use, because the shelf life (the time a paint remains in a good state for use) varies considerably from pigment to pigment. For example, Vermilion will harden in the tube in only a fortnight if ground with linseed oil, as I have found to my cost. From early days Vermilion was ground with some kind of wax to stop it drying so rapidly.

Today it is safe to say that the artists' colourman (the manufacturer) has tried to iron out the problems and variations of each pigment so your paints will behave – in terms of drying and shelf life – in the same manner. Of course there will be variations – Ivory Black will remain a slower dryer than other paints – but if you stick to the lists on p. 14 you will encounter few technical problems.

I use Artists' professional quality oil colours, but these are expensive, so I recommend you use Rowney Georgian oil colours. These paints are produced so the quality is as high as possible, whilst the price of different colours remains constant. I used Georgian oil colours for most of the demonstration paintings in this book.

Medium (plural media) refers to the different types of painting you can do, i.e. oil, acrylic or watercolour.
Medium (plural mediums) describes the additives which the artist uses with a paint to make it behave differently (e.g. turpentine is added to make the paint run more easily).

9

WHAT EQUIPMENT DO YOU NEED?

Your requirements can be very simple. When you choose anything, ask yourself two questions: is it reasonably strong so it will stand up to a lot of wear and tear without breaking down; is it essential, i.e. will it make painting more comfortable or make you more efficient. You will find you will collect endless things which are sometimes useful but you could do without. Every now and again, turn out the room in which you paint – be ruthless. I speak from bitter experience, because I collect far too much which I like to look at and, if I am honest, use once in a blue moon and could well do without.

On p. 8 you can see a paintbox, which you will find very useful. A container for holding your paints is essential; it does not matter if it is an old attaché case or a beautiful mahogany box like that. I have several boxes; the one I like best is an old, cork-lined one which I acquired, full of butterflies, as a child and my father adapted for me when I was a student. It has the minimum number of divisions for brushes, paints, an oil tin and a turpentine tin and a device for saving paint, and it also holds a 25.4 × 35.6cm (10 × 14in) board in the lid. In the division for brushes there are palette and painting knives, two dippers and some drawing pins and a paint rag (there is another rag on top of the tubes of paint). Whatever box you choose, old or new, make sure it is long enough to hold your brushes and not too heavy if you are going to paint outdoors. The combined easel and paintbox is lovely to look at but I find it requires too much hard work if I want to walk some distance.

When I go out painting I sit on a chair or stool. The one I like most is an army surplus chair with a back so I can lean back comfortably. I have tried out most chairs or stools that are available, the only one I do not like is the tiny folding metal stool, because it gives me a cramp in my thighs. Your stool or chair should be strong, easy to carry and not too heavy. Do not choose a comfortable, lightweight garden chair which is fine for sitting on but has arms which restrict your movements when painting.

In the studio I use a tall chair with a back (the sort which was used by counting office clerks). It is comfortable and my head is approximately the same height as when I stand. This means I can do a drawing sitting down, and later, when I stand to paint, I see the objects or my sitter from the same height. I keep my palette beside me on a tall kitchen stool, so it is easy to mix up my paints. Many of my friends use old tea trolleys or have constructed a series of compartments on wheels. The top level of the trolley can make an excellent palette – lay down some white paper and cover it with a sheet of plate glass cut to size. This is easy to keep clean and is a nice surface on which to mix up your paints.

If you like painting people, a 'throne' is necessary so you raise the level of your sitters in relation to yourself and do not always look down on them. Mine is 137.2cm ($4\frac{1}{2}$ft) square, 30cm ($11\frac{3}{4}$in) high and on castors so that it moves easily. An old screen is helpful; you can hang material over it to change the colour of the background behind your sitter.

You may have a spare room which you could convert into a studio. This would be ideal because it means you can leave things about and do not have to go through a clearing up session before you start to work. Also, I believe it is helpful to leave paintings around so that in unguarded moments you can glance at them and see what should be altered. I have worked in many different rooms and have found the only thing I am very concerned about is a good source of light. In the northern hemisphere a window facing north – a north light – is best because it produces the most constant light, whatever time of day you work (in the southern hemisphere the reverse is true). Do not have carpets on the floor, sooner or later you will spill something. I once dropped my palette on an Aubusson carpet with unhappy results! If you have to work in your sitting room or kitchen a large sheet of polythene for the floor is useful.

A EASEL
B PAINTING KNIVES
C PLASTER CAST
D LINSEED OIL
E SPARE CLEAN BRUSHES
F PAINT
G BRUSHES IN USE
H PAINT RAG
I SINGLE DIPPERS
J PALETTE
K PAINT BOX
L T—SQUARE
M RETOUCHING VARNISH
N TURPENTINE
O ADJUSTABLE MAGNIFYING GLASS
P DOUBLE DIPPER

Fig. 1

Brushes

There are three main types of brushes available: hog, which is fairly tough; sable, which is soft and springy (there are soft brushes made from ringcat, ox ear hair, squirrel and mixtures of hairs which are cheaper, but not as springy as sable), and man-made fibres, usually a form of nylon (some of the modern ones are very good and cheap). A good brush wears well and goes back to its original shape quickly. Sables are the most expensive.

Good brushes are essential when you start painting (see p. 27 for how to look after them). I recommend you purchase Round Hog brushes (Rowney series 111), sizes 1, 2, 3, 4, 5 and 7, two of each size. Round Hogs give you a greater choice in the kind of mark you make. (Round brushes are shown at the top of **fig. 1**, starting with the smallest.) Also buy two fine sables (Rowney series 134), sizes 4 and 5 (shown immediately below the Round Hogs). The next brush illustrated is a wide varnish brush (details on how to use it are on p. 64). There is a number of other shapes, from long filbert to short square brushes which you will find useful later. They are all nice to use and you should try them, but they restrict the kind of mark you can make. For example, a square brush makes a square brush stroke, which can be tedious if repeated in all your pictures. The shape of brush you enjoy using is a personal matter about which you should slowly make up your mind.

Painting surfaces

You can paint on a variety of surfaces, which range from very cheap paper to expensive canvas. The crucial thing to remember is that you want the oil paint to become one with the surface, but not sink in so all the vehicle (oil in the paint) is sucked out, leaving behind an unstable pigment which will brush off. For example, if you paint on ordinary cartridge paper the oil is rapidly sucked out and forms a halo round the paint – it dries almost immediately and is a very difficult surface on which to work.

In **fig. 1** there are some painting surfaces, including specially prepared paper for sketching, an oil painting board, a canvas panel, a stretched canvas, a piece of un-primed canvas and three different kinds of primed canvas. Oil sketching paper is the cheapest but is not easy to use because it is too smooth; you need to put a wash of paint on it first (this gives you a surface onto which your paint can join). Canvas can be made of cotton or linen and can be very smooth or very coarse (the best is linen). With a coarse canvas you will have to paint more thickly and leave touches of paint alone. I have painted on almost everything, from wood to canvas to paper. For large works I use canvas, for smaller works, boards. I recommend you use canvas panels at first because they have a 'tooth' which holds the paint and helps you apply it.

Fig. 2

Palette and painting knives

There is a double dipper shown in **fig. 2**; one half is used for cleaning your brushes, the other for holding your painting medium. The best to get is a 38mm (1½in) double dipper. Sometimes I use a single dipper – for example, when I am doing an underpainting in one colour. Palette knives, which have straight blades, are for mixing up your paint and cleaning your palette. Painting knives are more flexible and are cranked to facilitate putting paint onto canvas. There is a wide variety available. I have found the shapes illustrated the most useful – these are the knives which I used for the palette knife paintings discussed later in the book.

Fig. 3

Easels

An easel should be rigid and capable of taking the size of canvas or board on which you want to paint. It is useful if you can vary the height, you can then work more easily on different parts of the picture. In the studio you want an easel which can take a larger picture than you would normally work on outdoors. The studio easel illustrated at the left of **fig. 3** will take a maximum canvas size of 195.6cm (77in). I do not know who designed this easel in the first place, it was long ago, but it remains the universally accepted pattern for a studio easel – it is firm, not too heavy and can be folded up. I have painted larger pictures on such an easel with an arrangement of hooks and string to hold it rigid!

When you go out painting you will need a lighter weight easel. The one shown at the right of **fig. 3**, which I have known for many years, is the best available. It has the great advantage that you can sit or stand to paint (many portable easels do not allow you to do this) and will take a maximum canvas size of 127cm (50in). The head which holds your canvas or board at the top is reversible (one side is smaller for boards, the other is wider to hold canvasses). In windy weather, a string hanging from the centre, on which I hang my paintbox, ensures that the easel is perfectly rigid. Both these easels tilt so you can have your picture at an angle which does not reflect the sun.

RANGE OF COLOURS

You should skim through this page in the first instance, but refer back to it frequently. I have divided colours into groups denoting different degrees of usefulness. On the whole, it is better to use a small range of colours and explore what you can do with them. Devices such as a colour wheel will show you how you can get a surprising variation of colours with relatively few paints. Use another colour only when it becomes essential: i.e. the only red on your palette is Cadmium Red and you wish to paint a purplish-red object, so add Crimson Alizarin.

The basic colours

Flake White or Titanium White: Flake White has been used since time immemorial; it dries more quickly and has more body. I prefer it, but many of my friends prefer Titanium White. When I refer to White, I mean Flake White.

Yellow Ochre: This is a general purpose yellow. When mixed with White, it will become quite a bright yellow. It is a very useful colour in almost all mixtures.

Cadmium Red: This is a pillar-box type of red, which is necessary not only for red objects but also for warming up things (see pp. 30–31).

Viridian (Monestial Green): This is probably the most difficult colour to handle, but green is essential on your palette. Sometimes you want to make something greener, rather than bluer or blacker. Mixed with yellows, Viridian can make a lovely series of different greens.

French Ultramarine: This is the best general purpose blue.

Ivory Black: This is the blackest black. Think of it as a colour, not a darkening agent. Remember that Impressionist artists like Monet found it essential for most of their lives.

Colours which are sometimes necessary

These are colours which you will often find essential. For example, it is difficult to paint a lemon if the brightest yellow you have is Yellow Ochre.

Lemon Yellow or Cadmium Yellow: These will produce much brighter yellows in mixtures.

Crimson Alizarin: This purplish-red is sometimes essential, but a difficult colour to handle because it is apt to get into everything. Try using it and you will see what I mean.

Burnt Sienna: This is the best universal brown.

Cobalt Blue: It is hard to describe the difference between this and French Ultramarine, but I find Cobalt's gentleness generally more useful.

Cobalt Violet: Though you can make a violet with red and blue, this is sometimes necessary.

Colours which are sometimes useful

Cadmium Orange: This is a real orange colour.

Light Red: This strong brownish-red can be pleasant, but it is difficult to handle.

Coeruleum: Personally, I very seldom use this, but many of my colleagues find it essential.

Raw Umber: This is the fastest-drying colour and is an excellent colour for underpaintings.

Terre Verte: This is a gentle green which many people find useful when painting portraits.

Cobalt Green: A green which is not as harsh as Viridian.

This palette is set out from light to dark, for a right-handed artist. Note how much paint is put out

SETTING OUT YOUR PALETTE

It is important that you develop habits which save you time. The most obvious of these is to set out your palette in exactly the same way and to put each colour in exactly the same place each time. When I paint, I do not have to look to see where French Ultramarine is, my brush automatically goes to the same place. (Imagine a good pianist, his fingers go to the particular note he wants because he knows where it is without thinking.) In this way, I can concentrate on how much of that colour I want to take. Another point – this habit is helpful when you are working outdoors in a bright light or indoors in a dim one. It is very easy to confuse colours in such lights, thus wasting your time.

There are many ways of setting out your palette, but remember these basic rules. Any method you use should work with your kind of painting and should remain unaltered unless you make a major change of style. It should be sensible – do not go in for odd arrangements just because you think they look pretty on the palette; your palette is where the real work takes place. When you put a stroke of paint on your canvas, it should be the colour you intend, you should have worked it out to the best of your ability at that moment. Do not put colours on the bottom edge of your palette (the lowest edge in the illustrations). It is very hard to pick up the exact amount of colour from this area. Try it out for yourself and you will see that you will have to hold your brush in a different way and concentrate on picking up the colour. Even then, if your brush is splayed out, you will discover it is impossible to be accurate.

At the bottom of these two pages you can see two useful layouts which are the most helpful for you. On p. 14 you will see that the colours are set out in order from white to black (light to dark). In the corner is green, the warmer colours are on the top edge, the cooler colours (green, blue and black) are on the left. This is a useful layout if you are a tonal painter, i.e. tone holds your paintings together. I was shown this way when I first became a student and I have used it ever since. Note that the palette on p. 15 is set out for a left-handed painter. I am left-handed and many artists I have encountered are left-handed. The big difference in layout is that white comes in the middle and this layout is more useful if your main interest is in colour rather than tonal relationships. At the top are the warm colours (the lightest nearest to white) and at the side are the cool colours (again, the lightest nearest to white). If you favour this system, are more interested in colour and are right-handed, just reverse the whole thing and put the white where the green is in the photograph on p. 14.

This is an alternative method of setting out a palette, this time as a left-handed artist would do it. White is in the middle, warm colours are at the top and cool colours are down the side

CHOOSING YOUR SUBJECTS

In the first instance, choose a subject at which you like to look but, broadly speaking, there are four main areas of subject from which you can pick: still life, landscape, people and imagination. I have added palette knife painting as a fifth 'subject' because some beginners find they are a little timid or mean with paint when working with brushes. Whatever the subject, make sure it has a number of different coloured objects in it and it is not too simple. Paint the objects large; if they are too small you will have difficulty in manipulating the paint and the correct placing of each touch of paint becomes too important (see the two drawings at the bottom of the page).

Still Life with Mirror: Try painting objects you have just left on the table at the end of breakfast. Do not set up special still life arrangements. In this painting I wanted to explore tone – everything in the mirror is a little darker than it is in nature. I did not spend a long time setting it up but rather let the reflections in the mirror dictate the design. Note the size of the objects in relation to the canvas – they are quite big.

Brown Field: Try painting the view from a window of your home, *whatever it is like.* You will not have the problem of flies on a hot day or rain on a dull day. Even a brick wall can be interesting to paint. In *Brown Field* I did not bother at all about the design, but I was bothered by flies! I drew in a few lines to indicate the edges of the fields or clumps of trees and then started to paint. I worked out the relation of each colour to the one next to it in the landscape.

Still Life with Mirror, 63.5 × 76.2cm (25 × 30in). Collection of Vera Taylor

Brown Field, 20.3 × 25.4cm (8 × 10in)

The subject as shown below on the left would be fun to paint, but unless your board or canvas is very large the details of the town would be too difficult for a first painting (each object would be too small). I suggest that, given this subject, you paint the area within the dotted lines. The diagram on the right shows the scale of the objects as they could be on your board

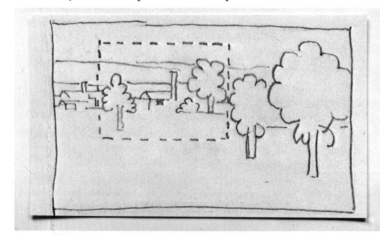

Miko Russell: If you want to paint people, get a friend to sit for you, but make sure he will not mind whether or not the resulting painting bears any resemblance to him. However much you may think a good likeness is essential, it is a problem to tackle later, when you have done a few paintings. Paint either a head or a figure in a setting. For the former you can work out the head in some detail, but in the latter keep the head and hands very simple. Miko Russell is a well-known musician and singer. I painted this in an Irish singing pub between bouts of tin whistle playing by Miko. This was one of the best exercises in concentration I have ever had! Note that I bothered a lot about the character of the head, but not at all about the painting of the jersey and the background, except to establish the colours.

Adam and Eve: Almost all the teaching in this book is concerned with observation and developing your visual imaginative responses – with painting from nature. Some of you will want to work from imagination. It is best to work from some sketches, however slight these may be, in which you think out the design you wish to paint. If this can be done from nature, so much the better. Try to think of variations on your theme and, better still, paint on several versions at once. *Adam and Eve* is a remarkable painting for an amateur artist. It is very well thought out in terms of design and took a long while to paint. It is large, and even if you think it is ambitious for a beginner, it is a good model for you to study.

Provençal Landscape: With a palette knife it is essential to ensure the scale of the objects is not too small. You must not fiddle and you will find it difficult to do so with a knife. A detailed description of painting with a knife is on pp. 60–63. Here, I want to get across the idea of it being a useful but different way of approaching your subject, rather than discuss how it is done. Painting with a knife lends itself to certain subjects more than others. This you must find out for yourself; I have some friends who paint every subject with a knife. It is useful to the beginner who gets bogged down or finds all his colours are rather muddy.

Your first painting: It is much better to 'have a go', to put down some paint and not bother whether you are doing it the wrong or right way. Gradually try to pick up good habits because they enable you to concentrate upon the ideas you want to express, but do not make a fetish of them. They are a means to an end, not the end itself. Draw your picture on your board with one colour (not black or white) and then paint.

Miko Russell, 45.7 × 35.6cm (18 × 14in)

Adam and Eve, by A. E. Webb, 91.4 × 121.9cm (36 × 48in). Collection of *The Artist* magazine

Provençal Landscape, 25.4 × 35.6cm (10 × 14in)

LET'S START PAINTING

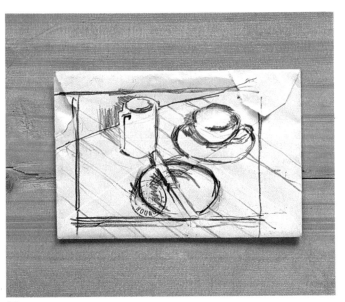

Fig. 4

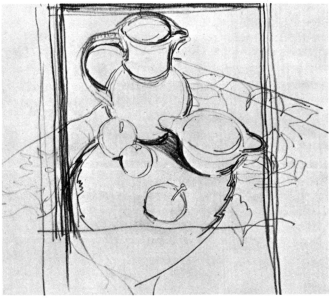

Fig. 5

DRAWING WHEN YOU PAINT

I said earlier that it is important not to worry about learning drawing skills before you paint. I am so insistent about this because more beginners worry about this than about any other subject when I meet them for the first time. I believe it is much more useful to develop skills as you go along because they become necessary. In other words, when you cannot improve any more until you do something about your drawing; then take time off from painting and make careful drawing studies. However, there are ways of using drawings to save you time which I want to discuss here.

Before you start painting you need to decide upon the extent of the subject you want to depict, and the shape and size of your support. Vary the size that you paint unless you have to produce a picture of a particular size (i.e. for a friend or an exhibition). Ideally, you should paint a small picture and then a large one. You will learn from both.

Make a diagram, rather than a drawing, on any old scrap of paper. **Fig. 4** shows a diagram I have made to sort out some points on the back of an old envelope. I drew the subject very roughly, looked at this diagram and decided I would concentrate as much as I could on the three objects. I drew in the lines of the shape of the painting board I had in mind and began to look more carefully at the shapes of the objects. You can see where I have 'looked' by the slightly heavier lines. Sometimes make several diagrams, thinking of different shapes; for example, whether you will paint an upright or horizontal painting.

On occasions you will find your subject seems to dictate a particular shape immediately. Even when this is so, have a look at it in other shapes. For example, a square painting is unusual but sometimes just what you want. At other times you will find you just do not know – then choose a shape arbitrarily and see what happens. In painting nothing is as useful as your own experience, but remember that a shape you find most unattractive on one occasion will on another prove to be the perfect answer – experience must always be tempered by experiment.

Both the diagrams on this page are slight. I am trying to use them as aids to thinking, not bothering about how good they may or may not be. Perhaps the marks made in the still life with a jug (**fig. 5**) show more clearly how I have changed my mind. Note how I have altered the upright lines, gradually bringing them in much closer. By the time I had finished this diagram I was clear on what I wanted to do and was able to move on to the painting. Both drawings led on to paintings in this book.

Once you have used your diagrams to decide the extent and shape of what you want to paint and the size of the

These are the sort of diagrams you will find useful. Do not fuss about them, do not show them to anyone, but regard them as private notes

Fig. 6

board you are going to use it is time to move on. Of course, you will gain something if you make your diagram into a careful drawing, but it is better, having solved the problems you set yourself, to start on the painting. A lot of nonsense is talked about how to draw on your board before you paint. In **fig. 6** you can see that I have run the whole gamut. On the left I have drawn in pencil, gone on to charcoal in the middle and then used one colour, French Ultramarine, and turpentine on the right.

Charcoal drawing like this is not a good way of proceeding. First, on a board with any grain or 'tooth' it is inaccurate. Does the thickness of the tree trunks I have drawn in charcoal extend to the edge of the charcoal mark, or is the tree described by the inside of the mark? Secondly, when you paint over such marks the charcoal is picked up by your paint, which immediately becomes grey. If there is a lot of charcoal the change of colour can be very marked. Some people try to 'fix' their charcoal drawing with fixative or by drawing over the charcoal lines with a sable brush dampened with a little colour and turpentine. Using fixative in this way is technically a bad method, whilst the latter is most laborious.

Drawing with a pencil, as in the left of **fig. 6**, is possible but not a good practice because the strong pencil lines will strike through the painting in the course of time. By far

the most useful way of proceeding is as I have done in the right of the drawing, using one colour and turpentine.

Many beginners seem reluctant to draw in this way on their board, but with practice it can be fun as well as efficient. When I am painting outdoors or when I am concerned most about colour, I find it helpful to draw with French Ultramarine or Cobalt Blue. You can vary the colour you use as long as you do not use Ivory Black because it dries too slowly and White or Yellow Ochre because they are difficult to see. A nice alternative is to mix blue with red, which will give you a cool or warm grey.

When painting indoors, or when I am working on a picture in which the design is particularly important, I use Raw Umber because it dries more quickly than any other colour and does not interrupt the subsequent layers of paint applied on top.

The secret is to paint with a thin sable, using lots of turpentine, to put the lines down firmly and, if they are incorrect, to alter them with a rag moistened with turpentine. You can learn to draw by taking things out or pushing them around with a rag.

Do not mix White with your colour for your preliminary drawing. Use the colour and turpentine only.

PAINTING IN TONE WITH
ONE COLOUR AND WHITE

Tone is the difference between the light and dark of objects when compared with each other. It is one of the qualities which you have to take into account when you mix up each colour. The others are the hue (red, green, blue or black) and the temperature (the relative warmth or coolness of objects compared with each other – this is discussed in some detail on pp. 30–31). When you mix up your colours on your palette it is a good plan to ask yourself three questions: What is the hue of the object? What is the tone of it compared with the surrounding objects? What is its relative warmth or 'coolth'.

Sometimes it is helpful to do exercises in which you deal with just one of these qualities; such as painting everything in three tones: light, half-tone and dark. The still life above has been painted in this way – compare it with the illustrations on pp. 22–23. I used Raw Umber, Flake White and turpentine. I put out on my palette large quantities of White and Raw Umber. I mixed some of each to produce as near a half-way house between the two as I could (fig. 7). Using these three tones, I painted the still life. It is a little stark but it is a useful way to sort out the main changes in what you paint.

A progressive exercise from this is to mix up five equal tones (White, a new half-way house, the half-tone, a new half-way house, Raw Umber). The most difficult exercise of all is to construct a scale of nine tones, the difference

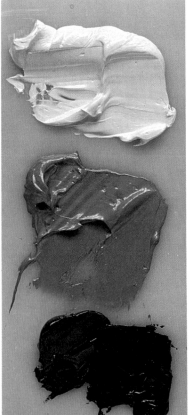

LIGHT

MEDIUM

DARK

Fig. 7

Devon Landscape, 25.4 × 35.6cm (10 × 14in)

between any two being the same as the difference between any other two. It is worthwhile doing this.

To return to the present exercise, you will find it makes you very aware of shapes. Some of you will discover that you rather like shapes, others may well be aware that the way objects become less distinct in contrast with each other as they move away from you (atmospheric tone) interests them much more.

If you examine *Devon Landscape* you will notice that I have varied the tones considerably – there are many more than nine tones and I have paid particular attention to small changes between one object and another. I used French Ultramarine and Flake White in this painting to emphasize that tone is *not* the difference between the colours black and white, but is the difference between dark and light. Get used to thinking of black and white as colours. You can darken or lighten most hues, but it is obviously difficult to lighten pure Flake White and darken pure Ivory Black. I am not indulging in semantics but trying to explain what is meant by tone.

Going back to the basic colours I have described on p. 14, there are some general rules about lightening and darkening colours. You can darken Flake White with every other colour; darken Yellow Ochre with Cadmium Red, and lighten Ivory Black with everything except French Ultramarine (you would notice scarcely any difference if you

mixed these together). For some of you, this will appear to be unnecessary theory but I would like you to grasp the importance of it when painting. For example, when you look at a landscape trees which are the same colour appear paler as they go away from you. There is a difference between the light and dark side of the trees in the foreground of *Brown Field* on p. 16; note how some of the distant hills are lighter in tone.

An awareness of tonal differences and an ability to paint in tone can be one of the most interesting aspects of painting. A judicious placing of tones can hold your picture together. If you look at the cartoons on pp. 48–49, you will see how I used large tonal drawings to help me sort out the design and shapes of the two pictures.

If you compare the tonal patterns of *Devon Landscape* and *Still Life with Blue Mug*, you can see the great difference in subtlety. If you place a dark on a light the contrast is stark, but if you place a dark accent in a half-tone area and make some gentle changes around it, the effect is more interesting. Suddenly you can emphasize a point by making a harsh contrast, such as the dark tree against the light wall on the left.

Tone is the difference between the light and dark of objects when compared with each other.

STILL LIFE STUDIES

Fig. 8

Every touch of paint has been considered. The final painting has been done on top of this

Fig. 9

Only the general mid-tone of each colour has been considered

A SIMPLE STILL LIFE

Not everyone likes to work in the same way. Here are two ways of starting a still life, both of which you have met before. What you have learnt on the previous two pages should be of help now. Remember, both methods are equally good and the one you use will be dictated by personal feelings rather than anything else.

In the painting in **fig. 8**, first I did a light tonal drawing in Raw Umber and turpentine. Then I mixed up my colours on my palette. I used a different brush for every change of every colour and mixed everything I was going to use. In each case I mixed a small quantity, not enough for use, but enough so I could see clearly what each colour looked like against the others. The purpose of this was to compare the colours I was mixing away from the objects and distractions such as drawing – was I on the right lines or should everything be slightly changed? At this point, it is very easy to start again, but later this is not so.

Then I began to paint, starting in the middle where a number of objects were adjacent to each other. I put down a small touch of the dark blue edge of the jug and placed against it a touch of the white of the cloth. Against that, the yellow of the cloth, then I placed a brown stroke – the edge of the plate. Quickly I moved over to the dark edge of the saucer and on to the lighter bit of the saucer, until I reached the dark shadow at the back of the cup. On this I placed the lighter brown of the cup. I built the painting up in this way (the finished painting opposite was done on top of **fig. 8**). Every touch I put down was important and I tried to make it the right colour in the right place.

The beginning in **fig. 9** has been done slightly differently. Very lightly, with a sable and Raw Umber, I drew the outline of the shapes of every object (these have been covered up by the paint). As carefully as I could, I mixed the general colour (the mid-tone) of each object. Finally, I painted these in quite swiftly. Every artist uses this method of painting from time to time, including myself. The only difficulty is that it presupposes you can judge the exact mid-tone – a feat that most beginners would find hard, but it is a good way of working which some of you will like. The next step is to paint the darker and lighter colours on to this mid-tone.

Opposite is the completed still life. I have worked deliberately and carefully and have tried to paint as close to nature as I could – putting touch upon touch, slightly modifying each area.

I used the basic palette – Flake White, Yellow Ochre, Cadmium Red, Viridian, French Ultramarine and Ivory Black – with the addition of Lemon Yellow so I could

Still Life with Blue Mug, 17.8 × 25.4 cm (7 × 10in)

make a brighter yellow. Please note that I have not used any brown and the Raw Umber has been used only in the underpainting or drawing. **Fig. 10** shows how I have obtained some of these colours. In each 'object' illustrated you will see there is a dark and light mixture, and in two cases, three. You will be able to see more than these in the still life. Study the mixtures I have made and practise making up colours in this way. It is surprising what you can achieve by varying the proportion of colours – often it seems you have made something quite new.

Mix colours on your palette, not your painting.

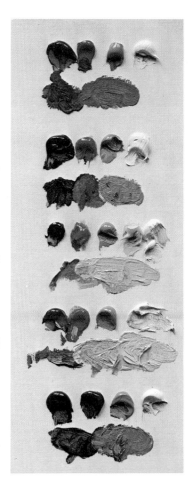

BLUE MUG

PLATE, CUP AND SAUCER

YELLOW CLOTH

WHITE CLOTH

WALL

Fig. 10

Fig. 11

Fig. 12

A MORE COMPLEX STILL LIFE

Remember the small diagram of a still life on p. 18? I would like to go a little further with that. **Fig. 11** is an underpainting which was done with Raw Umber and turpentine. I started by drawing coarse outlines of the jug, the edge of the cloth and the pot with a hog brush to see if I had got the scale right (I did not copy the diagram directly). When I liked this I began to develop each object a little more carefully. I used a rag dipped in turpentine to help me get the shape of the objects more accurately – you can see this in the apple nearest the front of the picture. I use this type of underpainting to have a good look at the subject – to notice what some objects are like against each other. I painted this in the evening by artificial light; shadows are particularly difficult in such a light and I wanted to think about them in advance.

This is not an accurate tonal painting (the apples are much too light against the cloth, for example), but a development from the diagram on p. 18 observing everything with greater intensity.

Generally, I start with the lightest colours, in this case the cloth, because they are nearest to white. I mixed the colour in the area just above the apple and below the brown bowl. Fix on a specific place and do not make a generalized colour. For the cloth, I used White, Yellow Ochre, Ivory Black and a touch of Cadmium Red. Later I added a little blue.

Then I went on to the apples. Both the warm and cool apples have been made with the same mixture of colours – Yellow Ochre, Cadmium Red, Crimson Alizarin (a touch), Viridian and White, but in different proportions. For the bowl I have used the same colours, with French Ultramarine instead of Viridian. Finally, I painted the jug with Viridian, French Ultramarine, Yellow Ochre, Ivory Black and White.

For each object I have mixed up three or four distinct colours, every time using a different brush; at this stage I was holding 12 brushes. Some of the colours were very similar – for example, two of the greens; and as I went on I used the same brush for more than one object. The purpose of so many brushes at the beginning is to try to analyse each colour clearly. If there are traces of other colours on your brush it is very easy to get muddled when you want to mix up a particular colour again. I added Lemon Yellow and Crimson Alizarin to the basic range of colours, and did not use Raw Umber as a colour. Some people will suggest that it would have been much easier to paint the bowl if I had used Light Red, but it is not an easy colour to handle, it is apt to get into everything in your palette, and we would never have found that such a rich brown could be made from those basic colours and Crimson Alizarin.

On the second evening I started painting from the centre

Still Life with Green Jug,
27.9 × 25.4cm (11 × 10in)

(the dark at the base of the green jug), gradually working out. In **fig. 12** you can see the point I had reached by the end of the evening. If you compare this with the final version you should note that the yellow cloth in the left foreground is too dark.

The next evening I spent a long time mixing up the same colours I had used before, *even though some were wrong.* You can see these colours in **fig. 13**. Practice in mixing up colours exactly is probably more helpful to the beginner than anything else – not as an abstract exercise but as a way of learning how to judge colours accurately. Then I went on with the painting. The following night I repeated the mixing and finally produced the finished painting you see above.

Think on your palette, put the results of your thoughts on the canvas.

JUG

APPLES,
WARM
AND COOL

BOWL

CLOTH

Fig. 13

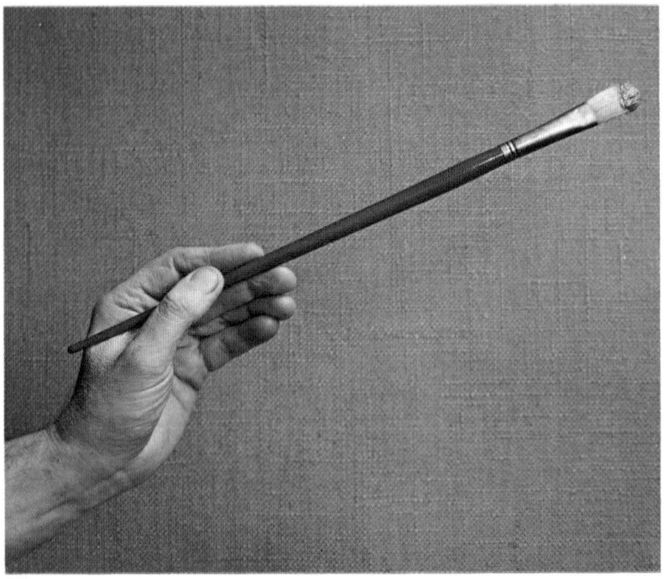

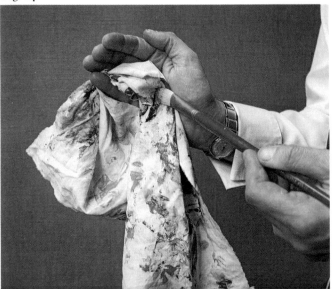

Fig. 14

BASIC TECHNIQUES

On these four pages are a few basic techniques you should master.

How to hold your brush

I like to hold my brush right at the end (see **fig. 14**) because this gives the greatest possible movement. Most of my friends prefer to hold their brush about half-way down the handle. Whatever you do, do not hold it on the ferrule near the bristles; easy movement is restricted and you will find yourself getting so near to your picture you cannot see more than a small portion of it and you will tend to hunch your back, which is bad for posture. Work with your arm extended as much as possible, this ensures you are well away from the picture and you will be able to see it as a whole and judge one part against another. Gainsborough used brushes 1.5 metres (5ft) long; I find it helpful to use 1-metre (3ft) brushes when working on large paintings.

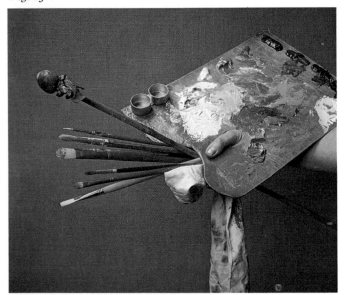

Fig. 15

How to use your paint rag

I mind very much about using brushes in good condition, but I have painted with brushes in an appalling state – they were loaned to me! I have never painted without some rag, even if it meant tearing off my shirt sleeve. The rag, which should be of cotton, not man-made fibre, is held looped over the little finger of the hand holding the palette. Use it by picking up part of the rag with a brush, putting it into the palm of your hand, closing your fingers around it and drawing out the brush (see **fig. 15**, but remember that I am left-handed). This has two functions: to clean your brush, in which case your fingers enclose the rag and brush firmly, or to bring paint down to the tip of your brush by pulling the brush through your closed fingers gently.

How to hold your brushes and palette

In **fig. 16**, as well as brushes and palette, I am holding a piece of rag and a mahl stick (this is rested on the edge of your canvas so that your painting hand with a brush in it rests on it; you can then put a tiny dot of paint in the exact place even if your hand trembles). At first when you try to hold your palette and everything else you will find it uncomfortable, but you will soon find it is more practical.

Fig. 16

How to look after your brushes

At the left of **fig. 17** are three brushes which have been rinsed in turpentine and then washed with household soap and water. The best way to get brushes thoroughly clean is to put some soap on the bristles and scrub them in the palm of your hand under running cold water (make sure you thoroughly rinse out the soap). The brushes will splay out after some use. To get them back to a decent shape, wrap the bristles with lavatory paper whilst they are still wet (centre brush) – as the paper dries it contracts and pulls the bristles back into shape. The brushes on the right have been subjected to this treatment and you can see how nice they look. Incidentally, the brushes on the left are clean, they have become a little stained with a dye colour. If you take care of your brushes they will last a long time.

How to stack your canvasses

Do bother with your boards and canvasses, both when they are new and after you have painted on them. When new, stack them as shown in **fig. 18**; so it is easy to see the sizes. You want to avoid bar marks on your canvas. If the canvas is good quality, you can get out damages by dampening the area of damage on the back; if the canvas is cotton it is impossible to get out such damages. When you have painted on canvasses do not stack them face-to-face, but facing the wall at a slightly steeper angle, to avoid spoiling the edges of your picture.

Palette shapes

Below are the two most sensible palette shapes you can get. The oblong palette (**fig. 19**) comes in a variety of sizes. Very small ones are not useful because there is not enough room on them on which to mix up your colours. The best size is 35.6×22.9cm (14×9in). The studio shape palette (**fig. 20**) comes in one size, 61cm (24in). It is curved so you do not have to stretch too far to reach your paint and to make it easier to hold. When you first buy a palette rub linseed oil into it for a few days before using it and when you clean it at the end of a day's painting. This stops the paint sinking in and gives you a nice surface on which to work. Flexible plastic palettes and 'tear-off' palette pads are also available, but these are not so good, except that they save you trouble when cleaning up.

Fig. 17

Fig. 18

Fig. 19

Fig. 20

Fig. 21
Fig. 22

Thick and thin paint

One of the great joys of oil paint is that you can work with it thickly or thinly. From the outset you should try to take advantage of this. Ideally, dark colours should be painted thinly and light colours thickly – they tell more. Every now and again, paint the very light areas as thickly as you can. This will be very obvious in your finished paintings, but you will find that with practice you will be able to make changes in thickness more subtle. If you have painted one area very thickly it is best to scrape it off with a penknife or palette knife if you want to paint over it.

From a technical point of view, you should paint from thin to thick, 'lean to fat' (see **fig. 21**). This is so that the underneath layers of paint dry more quickly than those on top (thick paint dries more slowly). But most people seem to think of thin paint as 'staining the canvas' which can be nice to look at, although it is not a useful way for the beginner to work. It is important that you put enough paint on your board or canvas because this will enable you to see if you are painting the right colour. If you paint too thinly the colour changes because of the drawing underneath.

Applying paint

There are many different ways of applying paint. The most dramatic difference is between using a palette knife and a brush. In **fig. 22** on the left, the brown mark was put on with a knife, all the others were done with a brush. These are your usual tools but you can also use your fingers (when Titian went on with a painting he often used his fingers) or the sharp end of your brush, but not too frequently. There are special fan-shaped brushes for blending edges. If you like using a great deal of paint, house painting brushes are best. There is a whole series of airbrushes, ranging from one that will produce a pencil-thin mark to others which will give a wide band of colour. You could try out some of these tools one day.

Let's return to your more usual implements. Each palette knife will make a different mark because it has a different shape. Broadly, you can apply the paint in thick bands or layers or small, thick touches. When using a brush, remember to keep the paint on the tip, not squeezed half-way down the bristles in an uncontrollable lump. You can put the paint on in very gentle touches when your brush skims the surface and only the paint touches the board. You can scrub it into your canvas with a dry brush; you can cover an area with rapid, thick strokes or slow, deliberate ones. There are only two ways you should not apply paint; as a house painter does, backwards and forwards over the same area, as this tends to make it lifeless and dull; or by mixing colours on your picture, i.e. adding a darker colour to a light one on your canvas and blending them together. Invariably, this will end in an unattractive mud.

Mediums and their uses

There are many mediums you can obtain easily from your local art store. If you look in one of the technical books on painting you will find endless recipes. Please do not use them, they will not help you paint better and most of them demand a complicated procedure which is of little advantage. All the reputable manufacturers make a paint today which is usable as it comes out of the tube. If you need to make the paint thinner (leaner), thin it with turpentine. One word of caution – many people are allergic to turpentine. If you find it irritates your hands or gives you a rash, do not use it. Instead use white spirit, BS 245 (mineral spirit), a petroleum derivative which behaves in a manner similar to turpentine. As you go on with a painting you should use paint with a mixture of linseed oil and turpentine, but never more than 50 per cent linseed oil (linseed oil will make the paint fatter). I tend to use paint with a little turpentine or on its own. Very rarely do I find it necessary to use the linseed oil and turpentine mixture.

When you are working with a dark colour which sinks (seems to go a dull grey colour), it is sometimes useful to revive it with retouching varnish. This brings back the colour you have painted, so you will be able to paint new colour accurately because you can see the old one clearly. Retouching varnish is useful as a temporary varnish for exhibitions. Do not go beyond these simple mediums.

DOES DESIGN MATTER?

On p. 17 I mentioned an excellent imaginative painting, *Adam and Eve*, which is a very good design. Some of you will be attracted to paintings in which the most important attribute is the design. Many European artists have worked in this way and probably the most helpful in this context is Raphael. The artists to whom design was all-important worked from drawings away from the subject. This book is about learning and observing from nature and is written for the beginner. It is easy to say that certain types of design work, and one should teach the principles of these, but all too quickly they develop into stereotypes. My main purpose is to show you ways in which you can advance, ways of criticizing your own work and ways in which you can teach yourself. Such a programme must be based upon *your* personal observations; the trouble with design is that it is based upon taste. It may be taste raised to the highest possible level, a major branch of art, but it is difficult to learn this except from a study of paintings and by reading commentaries or listening to lectures on them. This is helpful but should come a little later in your development. You can learn about design from nature and by criticizing your own paintings.

If you examine the way sea shells seem to go in a geometric spirals, the way petals seem to complement each other, and the way one part of a landscape leads you on to another, you will begin to see a certain order; an arrange-

ment of balancing shapes and forms; in short, the design inherent in nature. If you study this you will notice that one group of shapes pleases you whilst another does not and that certain objects make sharp accents that stop the flow of the movement around them. In art it is better to work from what you like than to accept a perfect model. I would like to find that one you happens to like curving shapes that flow into one another, that another you likes sharp, angular forms that jar, whilst yet another you likes variety.

A good design is one which tells the story which you want and makes the spectator understand what you are after. Do not think that I am writing about grand subjects, the rape of Helen and the fall of Troy. I am writing about small things, the silver trunk of that birch tree which shines out from the cool shadows around it, or the warm light which seems to embrace the piece of cloth and the apple on it.

Think of good design as a happy placing of things.

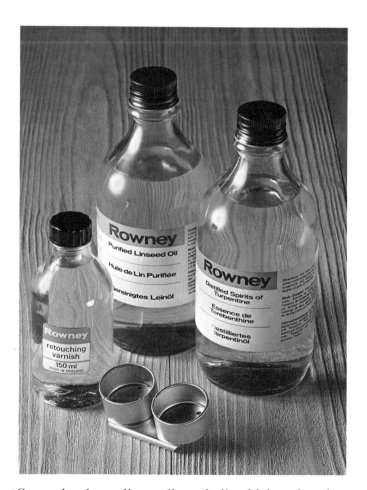

Some simple mediums: linseed oil, which makes the paint fatter; turpentine, which makes the paint thinner, and retouching varnish, which temporarily revives a painting

Fig. 23

Fig. 24

WARM AND COOL COLOURS

On p. 20 I suggested there were three questions you should ask yourself when mixing up a colour on your palette: What is the hue of the object? What is its relative tone? What is its relative temperature? It is an old, well-tried maxim that when painting you should limit your objective, say one thing well and not try to make everything perfect. If you can learn about one thing at a time you have a greater chance of solving that problem than if you try to sort out every aspect. French artists have always accused English artists (I do not think they included the Scots) of endeavouring to paint the perfect picture. Perhaps they were right in the past and you can show them that they are wrong now.

It would not be a bad thing for you to paint the same still life three times, each version devoted to one of the three questions I have suggested you should ask. The term hue is easy and I hope you now understand what I mean by tone. As for the third, the temperature of an object is its warmth and coolness in relation to the surrounding objects.

If you think of warm as going towards red, and cool as going towards blue, you will have made a good start, but do not worry too much if you do not understand the relevance of this. I must confess it confused me greatly as a student. Read through this section and come back to it later. Look at the two illustrations on your left, **fig. 23** is brown, yellow and orange, **fig. 24** is green, blue and grey. The top could be called a warm painting, the bottom a cool one.

In each painting some of the colours are warmer or cooler than others. For example, the yellow jug is not as warm as the orange, but the orange, although it is the most intense colour, is not as warm as the cloth on which it sits – the cloth is much redder. Which would you say is the coolest colour in this painting? It is the right side of the small jug which is a bluish-red. Below, the cloth is not as cool as the blue glass, but is the blue glass cooler than the green bottle? I think it is, because there seems to be a reddish cast in the green. The apple is certainly warmer. The warmest colour is the dirty wall at the back. If you transferred this wall to the top painting it would be the coolest colour there.

I am discussing relative values all the time. It is possible to paint the same subject twice so that each picture looks very accurate but one painting is warm and the other cool. It will depend on the emphasis you place upon certain colours. It is helpful to put up in front of you all the pictures you have painted and try to spot whether they

Lady in Richmond,
55.9 × 45.7cm (22 × 18in)

Irish Landscape,
12.7 × 19.1cm (5 × 7½in)
You can see here how a
contrast, the warm roof,
sings out against the cool
surroundings. Your eye is
drawn to that spot
immediately

have a tendency to be warm or cool. It is most likely they
will be coolish, most painters tend to paint in that direction
in the beginning. If this is so in your case, make sure you
push the warm colours in your next picture. A good
exercise is to set up two still life studies, not too complicated,
one predominantly warm and one predominantly cool.

Artists contrast cool and warm colours against each
other. I had fun with the quick sketch, *Lady in Richmond.*
The red of her jacket, though intense, is not as warm as her
cheeks; the blue in the background has a lot of red in it.
Even the black hair seems to be a warmish black, but the
warmest reds are her cheeks. This makes them much more
important. You may think they are too warm for your taste,
but I hope the painting gets across the message I want.

*The temperature of an object is its warmth or coolness in
relation to the surrounding objects.*

NOTES ON DETAILS

Fig. 25

Fig. 26

Fig. 27

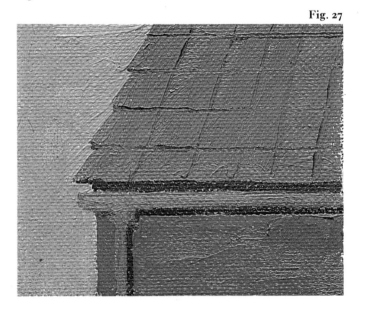

For some reason, almost every beginner thinks he must try to simplify what is in front of him, that it is essential he does not copy what he sees. The result of this is that he simplifies in the most obvious way, so his picture looks exactly the same as his neighbour's. It also happens that small areas of detail control the behaviour of the large forms. For example, the relationship between the wrist, elbow and shoulder – the points of articulation – fixes what the forearm and upper arm can do. If these points are well related, the arm will work, even if it turns out to be a little too thin or fat. These points of articulation are most obvious in a human being, but they are present in the whole of nature if you look for them and train yourself to notice them.

In general, it is better to paint all the details you can see, but always try to relate the scale of the detail to the scale of your painting. You may well be painting a landscape in which you can see a myriad of leaves upon trees in front of you, but you are working on a small board. Your trees are not large in the painting and the leaves you can see, if you paint them in scale, will be smaller than a pin's head. In such a small painting, you would have to sacrifice the detail.

Here are three of the most glaring examples of the kinds of details which are generally painted incorrectly and in which the scale compared with the whole is often wrong. **Fig. 25** shows the glazing bars of windows. Almost everybody forgets that with this type of sash window the top half is not in the same plane as the bottom half – it is set behind the bottom if you are inside or vice versa if you are looking from the outside. I have painted a fairly simple window to show how this appears where the top and bottom join – you could call this the point of articulation.

I have painted some bricks (**fig. 26**) to illustrate two different types of bond. There are many others but these should suffice to make my point. First, I would like you to notice that they are different. Second, note that the cement is lighter than the bricks (rarely will it be darker). Third, note that each brick varies. If you are painting a house made of bricks do not try to indicate the bricks unless you take the trouble to sort out the particular bricks and bond. Unless your painting is very large it is better to describe the general colour of the wall and not indicate the bricks individually.

Fig. 27 is an illustration of a tile roof. Note how it extends beyond the wall, that it is dark below the last row of tiles before you reach the gutter and that the size of each tile works in relation to the size of the roof.

DO'S AND DON'TS

PAINT AS MUCH AS YOU CAN FROM NATURE

DO NOT CHANGE WHAT IS IN FRONT OF YOU (I.E. DO NOT MOVE A TREE FROM ONE SIDE OF A LANDSCAPE TO ANOTHER TO MAKE A BETTER DESIGN)

MAKE LOTS OF SKETCH NOTES TO WORK OUT SOMETHING YOU DO NOT UNDERSTAND AFTER YOU HAVE BEGUN A PAINTING

PAINT OVER OLD PICTURES, BUT NOT ONES WHICH ARE TOO DARK IN TONE, VARNISHED OR RECENTLY PAINTED

ALWAYS MIX YOUR PAINT ON YOUR PALETTE, NOT ON YOUR PICTURE

USE A PALETTE KNIFE IF YOU FIND YOU FIDDLE TOO MUCH WHEN MIXING COLOURS ON YOUR PALETTE WITH A BRUSH

USE RETOUCHING VARNISH IF YOU NEED TO FRESHEN UP PAINT BECAUSE IT HAS 'SUNK' OR GONE DULL WHILE YOU ARE WORKING

IF YOU WISH TO USE A SERIES OF GENTLE COLOURS FOR YOUR PAINTING, CHOOSE THEM CAREFULLY ON YOUR PALETTE AND FIRMLY APPLY THEM TO THE PAINTING

DO NOT PAINT TOO THINLY

DO NOT FORGET TO TAKE CARE OF YOUR BRUSHES

NEVER BE WITHOUT A PAINT RAG

LANDSCAPES

LANDSCAPE PAINTING ON THE SPOT

This is the first demonstration in which I want to show you a number of stages so you can follow the painting through from beginning to end. I have chosen a landscape because everyone wants to paint the countryside at some time or other, and for many it is the starting off point of their interest in painting. *Distant Hills* is a simple landscape, there are no difficult details to draw and you could handle the painting in many ways. The different stages through which the painting goes were not, in practice, clearly defined, but have been chosen to make a point. The painting, which should be called a sketch, was done on the spot in one sitting which lasted about three hours.

The drawing This has been done with French Ultramarine and turpentine on a white board. When painting landscapes on the spot, I prefer to draw with blue rather

SKY

DISTANT HILLS

NEAR TREES

BROWN FIELDS

GREEN FIELDS

than Raw Umber because the colour is sometimes helpful and it does not matter if it grins through. First, I drew in the horizon line and the base of the large central hill. Then I began to work out the lines of the hedges as they came towards me and then the width of the horizontal fields. I put a tonal wash over the distant hill and worked in masses rather than lines. The purpose of this was to establish the main areas of trees and darker tones so that I began to get the sense of the space of the misty landscape onto my board. I wanted to get down the misty light of the sun striking through the clouds. The areas within the light changed so often that it has been more a question of establishing the general 'feel' of the landscape and noting one or two key points, rather than fixing the place of everything. The drawing has been left very loose, as time was pressing and I wanted to mix up my colours.

Mixing the colours I cannot emphasize enough that it is on your palette that you mix your colours, it is on your palette that you think and it is on your painting that you put the results of your thoughts. Trouble taken when mixing up your colours is always worthwhile. On the bottom of p. 37 you can see the palette I have used and the order in which I have mixed up the colours. Here I want to discuss the colours rather than the order. On the left you can see some of the mixtures I used. They have not given me all the colours in the painting, but they have given me the range in which I would work. The other colours are variations of these or could be mixed up between these on my palette. At the top of the illustration you can see the colour I mixed for the sky. The mixture for the lighter part in the centre of the sky, at the top, is not illustrated; for that I used White and Yellow Ochre, with touches of French Ultramarine and Cadmium Red. I knew I would start to paint where the sky and distant hills met, carefully relating these together. I mixed up the distant hills next, paying special attention to the differences between the warm and cool colours. All these colours are quite pale, so I turned to the darkest colours, the near trees. Then I made sure I had got the brown fields right, but note that the dark I have mixed up here is too dark. Finally, I did the green fields, but note here that these greens are altered later. I was then ready to paint.

First stage The first colour I put down was the darker part of the distant hill, against which I put the sky. Note that I drew over the hill colour with the sky colour to get the shape right – you can see this on the right. Also note that the blue drawing shows through in several places. Then I began to move towards the front of the painting,

The drawing

First stage

Second stage

putting down blocks of colour against each other, each time endeavouring to put them in the right place. I did not try to finish any one area, but put down a series of 'thoughts' in relation to each other.

Second stage The most obvious difference you will see between the first and second stages is that the sky was taken further and appears much lighter. I painted the areas which I had not touched, and the covering up of the white board makes the previous touches appear lighter, even though they have not been altered. Then I began to develop the sense of distance. For example, if you look beyond the row of green trees in the middle-distance on the right, you will see I have worked a lot at the base of the hill. I have introduced some pinkish blues and modified the dark colours on the hill. Next I worked on the five big fields near you, lightening the greens and changing the colour of the brown field. Notice how many touches of paint are beginning to draw each tree or field a little better.

Final stage Everything has been taken a little further. The clump of trees on the top of the hill were painted and some lighter touches were put into the sky. More paint has been put on the distant hills and all the trees have been modified. I spent most of the time working out the colours and shapes at the base of the large hill because they were very gentle against each other. Also, the subtle changes – a slight change of colour, not tone – were difficult to see in the bright light in which I was painting. (When working outside in a bright light I find a hat with a brim necessary to shade my eyes as I look at the landscape. I hold my palette at an angle so it does not reflect the light.) Small changes such as these can only be worked out in the best place – on your palette.

You can see my palette as it was when I had mixed up all my colours. Remember that I am left-handed; if you are right-handed hold the book up to a mirror and you will see the colours as you ought to set them out. By the time I had finished painting it was not so tidy. Each change of colour or tone I mixed up in the appropriate spot, so there would be various different shades of, for example, sky colour, occupying that space.

At the top of this page there are two details of this painting. The left one shows how the house blends into the surroundings so you do not notice it at first sight. On the right I hope you will see how I have changed an amorphous mass of colours into a group of trees and fields. This is what I mean by drawing – not, you will observe, a linear outline which is filled in.

If you look at the final painting you will see that I have been all over it, slightly changing everything. This is not mere eccentricity but a very useful way of ensuring that you think of each part in relation to the others. You will remember that this picture was painted on the spot in one go, and I cared most about the sense of distance and the misty light. The last few touches, changing the hill and modifying the light below the hill, mattered very much. When you do this kind of sketch always try to give yourself some time at the end so you can make little corrections all over it. Hurry to begin with, paint as if there is no time at all, so you leave yourself time to think of the whole. Do not try to repaint everything; look and see if there is a touch of paint which would help, not so much to complete a detail, but to express the idea more clearly.

Sometimes you need to add red to a green to warm it up.

Final stage

Distant Hills, 22.2 × 30.5cm (8¾ × 12in)

My board was a little too large, so I have put a wash of Raw Umber at the bottom so there was not a glare from the white board. This was cut off with a sharp knife when the painting was dry

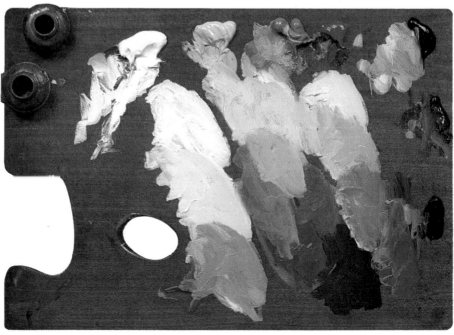

This is what my palette looked like when I had mixed up my colours. Remember that I am left-handed, hold the book up to a mirror to see how you should set out your colours if your are right-handed

A LANDSCAPE TAKEN FURTHER

The previous demonstration was concerned with painting a landscape in one go on the spot. Here I want to discuss taking a landscape painting further, working on it on several occasions. *The Beehive* was painted in four days, starting each day at 3.45 in the afternoon. I also made some corrections when I got the picture back home and I could see it without distractions. Each sitting lasted approximately two and a half hours. It was not possible to photograph the painting whilst it was underway, so I have reconstructed it and painted the stages again. Since I worked on such clearly defined occasions (when the afternoon was waning until it was time for an evening meal) it has been possible to do this accurately.

The drawing The painting was done on a red-brown ground and the drawing on top has been made with French Ultramarine. The main interest of the painting centres on the tree in the left foreground, the field beyond and the hedge on the right. To put this in context I was concerned about what went on behind, for instance, how the movement of the hedges encloses the foreground. Note how I went over the hedges several times in the drawing stage, making a tree on the right follow the shape. I have used a fairly wide brush because I was trying to work out the big shapes rather than paint a lot of details. At the end of the first session I blocked in the sky area quickly with some Flake White.

The drawing stage here was used not only to put the things down in the right place, but also to help me think about the best way to paint the picture. I chose to paint this because I liked what I saw, but it did matter what I put in the painting, i.e. I did not want to include the endless lovely landscape surrounding me but wanted to concentrate on the main subject, this is why there is not more sky. The hills rose up ahead and I was more aware of the landscape than the sky. This may sound a little difficult for you because you may not be as sure as I appear to be about the shape of the painting and what you might want in it. Do not forget that always it is better to make up your mind; to decide one way or another what you would like to have in a picture before you start.

I have heard much talk of 'artistic licence' and that the subject would look much better if you moved a tree or a building just a little way to the left or right. *Please* do not take any notice of this false advice – do not alter what is in front of you. Nature is lovely and it is your business as a painter to understand it – to find the design in what you see, not to think you can improve on it. Also, when you move something you leave a gap which is not easy to fill. It is important that you are able to judge one bit of the painting against another, and it is not a little difficult to do this if you introduce a new feature.

First stage On the second day I spent a long time sorting out the colours. This reconstruction shows the stage I had reached at the end of that day. I do not seem to have pro-

The drawing

38

First stage

**Detail of
second stage**

gressed very far, but I have been more interested in mixing each colour as I wanted and putting it down very freely. If you compare this with the final painting, it is clear I have been much freer in the early stages than I have been in the final version. Since I was most interested in a special area of the painting and since the way I thought about the hedge demanded working in great detail, the painting inevitably became tighter and tighter.

Do not be afraid of detail or of people who talk about 'knitting'; what they are describing are pictures where every mark and change, every detail can be seen. I would rather say: paint as meticulously as you can – try to look at every blade of grass, every twig and every branch, but always in relation to the scale on which you are working.

The building on the left is, in fact, a grand antique medieval beehive from France. If you compare the first stage with the detail of the second stage and the final painting, you can see that the right side changes tone through the different stages. It is a dull grey in this stage; a brighter yellow in the second stage and brighter still in the final stage. If you paint over a period of four days the light can change – it did very dramatically whilst I worked on this. It is always better to change what you have put down in front of nature because she has changed, unless you believe you have painted an object perfectly. In this case, it was not until the last day I realized how helpful it would be if that building were very light.

The fact that the light changes constantly should be thought of not as a nuisance, but more as a challenge. You should ask yourself: Is the subject I am working on better in a bright light or in a dull glow? In a bright light I could see many details which were hidden; should I have painted them? The distant fields seemed at one moment to be a brilliant brown, and at the next a dull, greyish green; which is correct? All possible permutations of the answer could be right in a picture, but they will not all be correct at the same time (some cancel one another out). It can be fun to choose; painting is not a mechanical exercise in which you follow a set pattern, but an adventure in which you can turn in many different directions, *all* of which are worthwhile.

It would be instructive for you to compare each point in the above stage with the final version. For example, the brown field in the centre background becomes much cooler in the final version, and the field below it becomes more blue and much lighter.

Second stage I have shown a detail of this stage so you can see what I have been doing clearly. Do not forget that it is useful to think of *every* brush stroke as a new idea, requiring you to modify your first mixtures. Has the new brush stroke a little more blue or red (is it warmer or cooler) than your original mixture? Make a decision to go one way or another. The near tree and hedgerow are much too blue, as I went on I noticed that they were much more interesting greens. By now you have probably realized that the correct

Final stage

The Beehive, 35.6 × 45.7cm (14 × 18in). Collection of Chris O'Neill

mixing up of colours is difficult. How often have you said: 'I can see the colour but cannot mix it up.'? Although it is difficult, this is where you should spend the most effort. Always be willing to change anything and always try to put down each colour as correctly as you can.

Final stage This painting aims high in that it forces us to make judgements about detail and subject. It is never useful to aim low; always try to make each picture you paint a little more difficult for yourself – do not fall back on learning how to do it one way. This is very different from *Distant Hills*, but it was painted within a short distance of it. In the detail of this stage (opposite, top) you can see how I have worked hard on the tree, it changes colour many times and the aim has been to sort out the groups of leaves. Carefully I watched where the darker accents in the tree appeared. It is easy to lose your place when you are working unless you fix on a particular spot for each brush stroke. This is even more apparent in the detail of the hedge-row, where you can see I noted the big shapes of the larger bushes and then worked into them (opposite, bottom).

In the left foreground, the muddle of post-and-rail fences caused me much trouble. I found it difficult to see what was happening. I used the tall post between the beehive and the main tree as a key; it caught the light whereas they were in shadow.

I made the large trees in the hedge work as I went along. You can see how I have drawn the branches of the tree by painting the field. In the final painting I have corrected these – do not try to do such details too quickly. It is more helpful to move on from area to area just before you have solved how to deal with each one. Leave the last brush stroke, paint elsewhere and then come back with a fresh eye and see what needs to be done.

You can make lovely greens by mixing black with yellow.

NOTES ON TREES

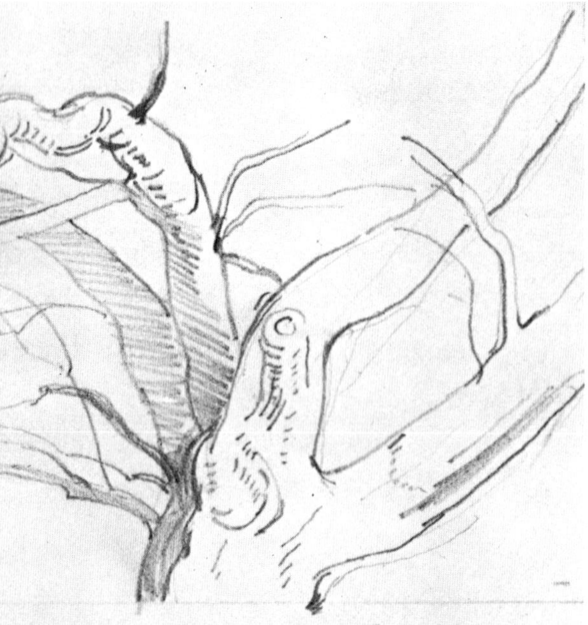

Fig. 28

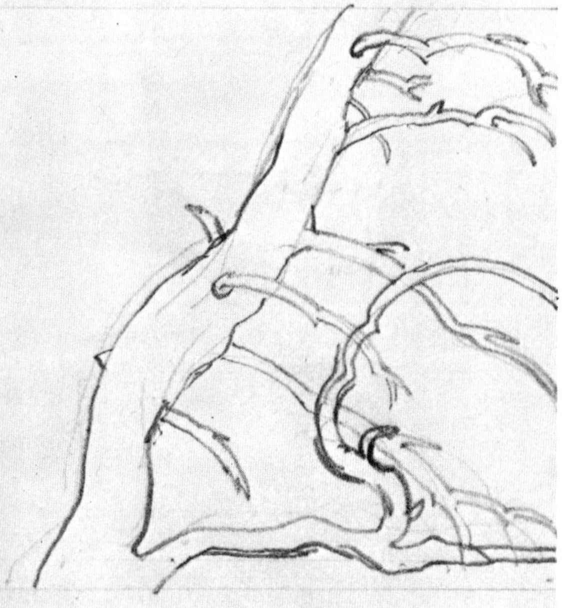

Fig. 29

Fig. 30

The illustrations on these pages have been drawn the size you see with a 2B pencil. Always, when you paint, you need information, and these are the small notes you could make when looking at trees in the winter. I was trying to make quick sketches of different types of trees which I could use in later paintings. My theme, as you will have gathered, is observation, and trees are something you can look at easily. Such sketches will help you remember small changes in the way an individual tree behaves. Trees do follow general rules, but it is more useful to think of them as individuals. There is only one tree that I find impossible to like – the coniferous fir that grows in endless forests all over the world. Its shape is unsympathetic, hard and un-yielding. However, I do like paintings of them by the German artist Albrecht Altdorfer. You will not be able to find his paintings easily, but do make an effort to look for some reproductions in a book – his work is well worth looking at.

Whenever you paint any tree there are certain basic things for which you should look. First, the silhouette; if you know the characteristic shape of a tree it will enable you to recognize one a long way away, but beware because trees do not always behave in character. I remember painting some willows that were very tall – we usually think of them as being pollarded and short. I remember searching in vain for an oak which grew in a semicircle, as the books I had read told me. Most oaks I saw seemed to be very old and grew in a most peculiar way.

Second, look at how the main trunk of a tree enters the ground. The two you see here, the pine in **fig. 30** and the walnut in **fig. 33** hit the ground quite differently. These are two extremes; most trees do not expand like the walnut, but enter the ground more like the pine does.

Third, look at the skeleton of the tree and see how your particular one grows. This is difficult in high summer, but you can see what happens if you walk under the branches to the centre. You should study how the branches split off from the main trunk. **Fig. 28** is a pear tree, you can see there are four major divisions from the main trunk at the same point. This is unusual and is generally due to heavy pruning. **Fig. 29** shows a fir where all the branches grow from one side. A strong prevailing wind stops a tree growing; its branches will only appear on a sheltered side. Fir trees have a main trunk; the branches spring out of this and both become thinner as the tree grows higher. The pear tree, on the other hand, divides more equally, though one branch will tend to be dominant. **Fig. 31** is an old walnut and here you can see clearly that each time a branch divides, one is still slightly thicker. Branches have been cut off this apple tree (**fig. 32**) and it seems to send out new branches at right angles – the pear seems to grow upwards.

Please pay special attention to how a branch joins onto the trunk.

There is an old idea, which appears to have been recorded first by Leonardo da Vinci, that the volume of the trunk equals the volume of all the twigs at the end of every branch. This belief was based upon the fact that when a branch divides the two new branches equal the old in volume. I am told by experts that this is not proven, but it is a useful precept for artists to follow. Every time a branch divides the two new branches will be smaller, but one will be larger than its companion.

How can you paint the skeleton of a tree in summer when it is covered with leaves? At times you will see branches peeping through these leaves. Make sure the branches you paint agree in scale with the way that tree might develop, even though you cannot see all the trunk. Constable found it helpful with trees to remove some branches of the trees nearest to you so that you could see the structure of the skeleton. For most beginners this would be difficult because it presupposes many studies. I would like to emphasize that these two pages are designed to show you how important studies of this nature can be.

There are two other important considerations when you paint trees. Try to think of your tree as umbrella with lots of holes in it, the ribs are the skeleton of the tree. You can see what is happening on the other side through the holes. Think of the way the direction of light from the sun makes one side of the tree light and the other dark. Because of the spaces between the leaves you can see dark areas on the light side and light areas on the dark side. Work out the relevant tone and think of the 'holey' umbrella.

Finally, look at the way that leaves group themselves together; each type of tree works in a different way. When painting, notice how these groups form patterns which are characteristic of that type of tree.

Much of this you can sort out by making the kind of sketches I have shown on these two pages. The more you can add to your store of knowledge the better, i.e. make sketches of the skeleton in the winter, even though your main interest may be in painting summer trees.

Trees are individual, as full of character as people.

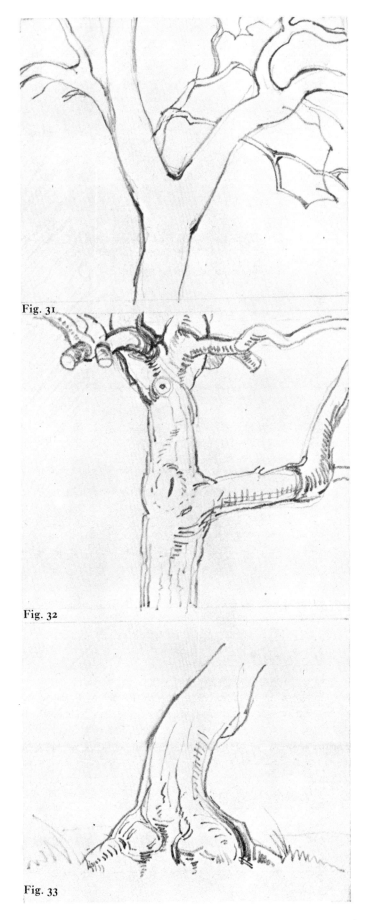

Fig. 31

Fig. 32

Fig. 33

PORTRAITS

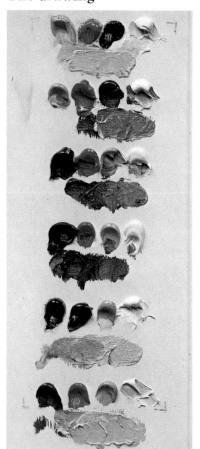

The drawing

LIGHT FACE

CHEEK

HAIR

CHAIR

WALL BEHIND

T-SHIRT

A PORTRAIT SKETCH

Contrary to popular belief, the way you paint a subject differs only because of your commitment to it, not because it necessitates another way of painting. In other words, you do not approach a landscape any differently than a figure, there is no special way of starting. Because we care more about some subjects than others, we tend to fight shy of those with which we have the least sympathy. I have maintained always that I learn as much about painting portraits when I paint a landscape as I do when I make a special portrait study. Since the kinds of colours in which I am involved are almost complementary (cool reds in portraits and warm greens in landscapes), I find I learn a lot about painting landscapes when engaged in portrait painting. It is true that when I paint landscapes I tend to do it outside, and when I paint portraits I tend to work on them in the studio.

With landscapes, I find it helpful to draw on the canvas in blue, with portraits I use Raw Umber. I have painted many portraits in which I have drawn in blue and landscapes in which I have drawn in Raw Umber, but as a general rule this does not apply because the design of the portrait usually has to be worked out very carefully – more about this later. *Judith* was done in one day – the photographs were taken from time to time when she needed a rest – and is a sketch.

The drawing It can be off-putting to start work on a board or canvas because of its whiteness (here I was working on canvas in the studio). Usually I stain the canvas with Raw Umber diluted with turpentine. I put it on the canvas rather coarsely and very quickly with a large brush. I wipe over it with a rag to make the tone more even and fill in any gaps I have left. Some people prefer to leave this Raw Umber wash more open and varied in tone.

I started the drawing stage by indicating the top of the head with a line, then I went to the edge of the hair on the right. I drew a line down the centre, where her parting would be, to the top of the centre of her forehead. Then I drew a line on the right down the edge of the face on to the chin and up the left side of the face. Quickly I massed in the tone of the hair with a big brush. At this point it is possible to see whether or not you have got the head in the right place on your canvas. If not, wipe it all out with a rag and turpentine and start again. If it appears correct, proceed.

The dark of the eyes (placing these fixed the scale of the head) was done with two coarse brush strokes, followed by the eyebrows, comparing the directions. I put in the line of the shoulders and the edge of the T-shirt around the neck, then came back to the right side of the face and corrected the cheek-bone and edge of the face. I drew in the right side of the nose, then the left, and moved down to the mouth.

Using a large brush, I put in the dark of the chair on the top left and corrected the top of the shoulders. I came back to the mouth, corrected its position and drew the line between the lips. The nose was not right, so I wiped out part of it with a rag and turpentine and then altered the line of the jaw on the left. I moved over to the right side of the face and changed the edge of the cheek-bone.

The purpose of all this was to get the head correctly placed on the canvas, to make the scale in relation to the size of the canvas sensible and to place the features. This is a quick sketch and I wanted to get on with the painting. (The drawing took about 20 minutes.)

First stage I used a different brush for every tone of every colour. I mixed up all the *basic* colours I was going to use (i.e. I did not bother with the colour of the mouth or the slight redness of the cheek). I put a little touch of each colour on the canvas, starting with the forehead (I have painted this too light), moving to the hair, the eyes and on. Each touch of paint was in the right place (or I should say as far as I could make it so at that stage). Every main colour was put down, sometimes with just one brush stroke. (This took about 20 minutes.)

Mixing the colours You will notice that I have spent as long on the first stage as I did on the drawing, although I have touched the canvas very little. Almost all the time has been spent in mixing up the colours on my palette. I have used the basic palette plus Raw Umber. On my palette, in order, were: Flake White, Yellow Ochre, Cadmium Red, Viridian, Cobalt Blue (instead of French Ultramarine), Raw Umber and Ivory Black. I mixed up the lightest colour of the face with Yellow Ochre, Cadmium Red, Viridian and White. I used the same colours on the cheek but I did try out on my palette the mixture I have shown you, using Cobalt Blue instead of Viridian. The hair was Raw Umber, Cadmium Red, Yellow Ochre and White, and for the chair I used the same series of colours in different proportions. The background used the same mixture as the chair, but without the red and I added Ivory Black to the mixture. I used Cobalt Blue, Cadmium Red, Yellow Ochre and White for the T-shirt.

Second stage For the next 30 minutes I worked on everything a bit more. I started to draw the eyes a little better, but did not paint the corners nearest the nose properly. More paint has gone on everywhere. Notes to myself: the drawing of the nose is askew and the corners of the mouth need some attention.

First stage

Second stage

45

Third stage

Third stage Never work on one area until it is complete at the expense of the rest of the painting. At this stage I was more concerned with getting the surroundings onto the canvas than with improving the face. It is a mistake to think that you can 'fill in the chair' or 'paint the background' whilst the sitter has a rest. You need her there so you can choose the right colours against her face. I sorted out the colours for the hair and began to get the colour of the T-shirt. Always have several tries at an object like a T-shirt; do not mix up the colour and paint it completely. At every stage I worked on the T-shirt a little, slightly modifying the tone or colour until I began to get it to my satisfaction. I corrected the left side of the face and then painted the chair.

It should be clear by now that although I try to put every brush stroke down in the right place, immediately I correct it with another stroke of paint placed beside or on top of it. I cannot emphasize too strongly that you should not use too much medium; you will find you can adjust a brush stroke more easily if you limit the amount of medium you use. (This stage took about 30 minutes.)

Final stage Everything has been taken a stage further, the T-shirt has been completed and the mouth made less disagreeable. Most people worry too much about the likeness; from these few reproductions you can see how the likeness changes and this is achieved by quite small alterations, for example, a touch to the edge of the mouth or the corner of the eye or nose. Try to get the basic structure right and make likeness corrections at the end of the sitting. In this case, Judith, my daughter, was growing tired and somewhat pensive. It would have been possible to make her smile by altering the corners of her mouth (cover them up with your fingers and you will see what I mean). I was more interested in getting her character down than painting her at her prettiest. (This also took me about 30 minutes.)

The sittings lasted just over two hours (she had rests at the end of each stage). It would have been possible to go on further, but if you want to paint a friend do not overdo the time you make her sit on each occasion. When I look back at the final painting there are alterations I would like to make, but what I notice most on the reduced scale you see is that it looks different from the real thing. The final judgement must be upon the painting you have in front of you. Personally, I found it helpful to stop here and leave it alone, but sometimes I like to get the sitter back to make an adjustment at a later date.

You can make orange with yellow and red; and mauve and violet with blue, red and white.

Final stage
Judith, 50.8 × 40.6cm (20 × 16in)

Detail from *Virginia and Sophie*

A PORTRAIT TAKEN FURTHER

The portrait *Judith* is a sketch and the design could be described as a 'happy placing'. *Virginia and Sophie* (p. 5) is a large, more considered painting, 106.7 × 134.6cm (42 × 53in), and the design had to be worked out carefully. I made a number of pencil studies rather like the envelope notes on p. 18. These gave me a rough idea of the size I would like to paint. The next step was the cartoon illustrated below. I used ordinary brown wrapping paper, charcoal and white chalk (this is a black and white photograph). I drew very rapidly, the exact size I wanted to paint. If you do this you can think out shapes on your canvas clearly. The lines ruled over it were duplicated on the canvas, which enabled me to copy the cartoon onto the canvas quickly and with the minimum of trouble (I used Raw Umber and lots of turpentine). You can do this away from the model.

With *Edwina* all the pencil sketches I made had been with the idea of painting a conventional upright portrait. Suddenly I noticed her reflection in a mirror behind her. Immediately, I started on a cartoon on the scale in which I wished to work, 76.2 × 101.6cm (30 × 40in). The chair

Cartoon of *Virginia and Sophie*, 106.7 × 134.6cm (42 × 53in). Collection of Jill de Brant

Cartoon of *Edwina*

and its reflection made a lovely shape in the centre of the painting and I was concerned about putting them in the 'right' place. If you compare this cartoon with the final painting you will see that the central figure is slightly smaller – the hands are not as near the bottom edge of the painting. I think of the cartoon not as a finished product which I copy, but rather as a step towards a picture which I will vary when I am painting. For example, in the cartoon of *Virginia and Sophie* I have not worked out the right side of the painting at all, and in *Edwina* the easel in the mirror was not considered.

If you use the envelope sketches and cartoon as aids to thinking out what you will paint, you will not need to worry about getting the drawing correct. Such cartoons are a way of sorting out your ideas privately. Although it may seem a long way round, I find it does save a lot of time in the long run and I can work away from the model. I stop working on a cartoon as soon as I have arrived at the main design. I do not use it as a means of studying the areas I know will be difficult, such as the hands. This method of working can be a real help if you stick to these ideas and do not feel the cartoon must be correct in every way.

The illustration of books is at the top right of the painting of *Virginia and Sophie*. When you look at the whole painting all you notice is that there are titles on the books – in fact the titles are all connected with the painting; where it was done and the date it was finished. I call this a 'conceit' and I enjoy having a little private fun in this way. Incidentally, when you sign your paintings do it discreetly so your signature does not interrupt the world you are making. This is even more important in small paintings. You can see in the detail of the chair on the next page where I have signed *Edwina*.

When you paint a more considered portrait it is worthwhile trying to make everything in it say a little more about the sitter. For example, I include the hands whenever I can because they say as much about the sitter as the face. You can see in too many distinguished pictures that the artist has painted the hands from another sitter, which is a bad practice.

The idea of using the mirror in *Edwina* was to try to give two versions of the sitter at once; the gentleness of her portrait looking at you, contrasted with the straighter-backed version in the mirror. When I have an idea like this, I think of the other reasons why I should do it. For example, it gave me another dress to paint which was slightly different in colour.

I knew when I started the painting that the dress was going to be difficult, I had no real idea how to paint it except I was determined not to do it sketchily. I had drawn the figure in Raw Umber and had put down the shape of the dress. I put down some of the darker blue strokes of paint, following the pattern as closely as I could. Into these I began to put some of the lighter areas. I noticed that the arm nearest the mirror was getting a reflected light from the mirror – I had painted this arm too dark at first but gradually lightened it. At all times I painted on the dress in the mirror whilst I was working on the main dress so I could watch carefully the changes of colour between the two and their relative values. If you choose to paint something like this, do remember that the dress you see in the mirror is the back of the dress you see in nature. I worked on the dress over several sittings, sometimes correcting bits after Edwina had left. This is only sensible if you can remember a correction you wanted to make but did not have time for when she was sitting – do not go on with it for the sake of getting the picture done.

I started with the head in the centre and had taken it quite a long way before I did much elsewhere. I have established the colour and tone of the chair behind this head, but did not do anything about the shape at this stage. Gradually, I began to work all over the painting. When you are engaged on a picture as complex as this you will work on one area alone and often forget there is a lot more in it. If you do this you are likely to paint that part out of tone with the rest. It is always sensible to mix up some of the other colours on your palette before you start, *even if you do not intend to paint with them.* At the beginning of a painting session, whilst I am mixing up colours, I think out exactly what I was doing before and what I intend to do now. As a beginner you will find this time invaluable. (Do make sure you have the same set of colours on your palette each time, otherwise you will get into an awful muddle.) When mixing up my colours I test them out on the painting to see if they are correct.

In the early stages of such a picture I do not paint on any part unless the sitter is there, it is too easy to get it out of tone. Later on it is possible to work on parts of the picture when she is not present. For example, I painted the right arm of the chair whilst she was there but the rest of it when she was not. I did a little of the pattern on the wall on the right whilst she was there but completed it when she was away. Invariably, I corrected such areas when she next sat.

In the detail of the chair you will see that each button is different and carefully painted but that I have not over-

Edwina, 76.2 × 101.6cm (30 × 40in).
Collection of Gareth Evans

stressed them – they had to be kept in a general dark tone but still add a little interest in that area. The curved bit of wood in the centre caused me a lot of trouble, I had painted it quite nicely but out of tone, so I scraped it down and started again. This does take quite a lot of courage for a beginner but it is well worth it – having done it once you can always do it again is not a bad maxim. The ability to take a lot of trouble has to be learnt and you will find that as you develop as a painter you are able to take more.

I have illustrated the detail of the hands in the mirror because it was an area of particular difficulty. First the colour, I spent a long while mixing up my colours on my palette, against the hands in nature. I wanted to get the sense of them being in a mirror; there is something different about them in a mirror, they do not look quite like hands in nature. The hardness of the light and dark on them helps a lot. I did not try to get these hands right on their own, but painted them over several sessions between work on other areas.

The reflection of the easel has been changed many times. At one stage I painted it in much more detail but it became too important and I had to lose the details. Often you will find this a helpful way to work; for example, the right sleeve of the dress in nature was painted in much more detail over a number of sessions, I simplified it because it detracted from other areas I wanted you to look at more closely.

Details can be lovely, only simplify something because there is a pressing reason to do so.

BUILDINGS

I have tried in this book to write about the sort of subjects that the beginner seems to like painting. Everything is paintable, even a plain brick wall, but you will always like some subjects more than others. Whatever you enjoy painting at the moment, it is quite a good plan to think about buildings, even if your main interest is in landscape – it will be rare if there are not some buildings around. On p. 32 I wrote some notes on the painting of glazing bars, bricks and tiles; these are of obvious importance when painting houses. On this page are two more details you should notice. Chimney pots on the skyline can be a nice accent in a painting. Think of the way they alter the silhouette, even though the large masses of chimney stacks stay the same they vary in shape quite a lot. Although there is not one in the study on the left, may I make a plea for television aerials, they work in a similar fashion. As for telegraph poles, they are even more useful in landscapes because they provide strong perpendicular contrasts against the horizontal countryside, which emphasize the roundness of the trees.

When you are painting chimney pots be careful not to get them too dark in tone against the sky. You see them as dark or light accents and it may be very easy to overdo the strength of this tone or colour. They are small, but you cannot fail to notice them if you get them wrong.

Below the chimney pots is a study of a typical London porch. Both these studies were painted the size they are reproduced because on many occasions they will be this size, or even smaller, in your paintings. Studies of this nature are well worth doing; they do not take long and give you a chance to have a good look. When working on small areas like this I find it much easier to keep the whole thing wet – to paint it all at once. You can see I have corrected the darker strokes of paint by pushing the light colours close up to them. When you paint details make sure the tops of windows and doors are square. Do not let them slope or leave them unfinished. Paint the darks first, then the lights. I work this way with glazing bars and finally correct them with the dark colours. I use a mahl stick and a small brush. I have painted these rather flat without very thick brush strokes. Sometimes it is fun to paint them much more thickly and rather more freely where only parts are indicated, but always make the corners of windows and tops of doors square.

If you look at the detail from *Sussex Landscape* you can see how I have taken trouble to paint the lower window carefully in this way. This is a detail from a larger painting, the rest was trees and bushes and does not concern us here. It was painted on the spot over two evenings. I like painting buildings and trees together this way. In the tree on the left you can see how several touches of the light building were painted on top of the tree – the light correcting the dark, but lower down the bushes were painted over the window and on the right the green leaves were painted on top of the orange building.

This is much more freely painted, with thicker paint, than I have used in the two studies opposite. There, I have eliminated almost all the brush strokes. Here I have painted in very definite touches. (I used no medium except to clean my brushes occasionally.) I keep trying to think of useful ways of working which might help you in painting details, but since I try to start painting as if I knew nothing and was seeing the subject for the first time, I can think of none that are useful. Except one overriding idea: Do not try to find an answer which will serve on each occasion, but learn that what is wrong behaviour in one picture can be the only possible answer in another. Every painting must be treated differently, indeed with a detailed subject, if you have worked one way more than once in a painting you *must* find another answer if that problem reoccurs.

Very often it will be the juxtaposition of a building with a tree which makes a landscape exciting to paint. For example, the particular orange-red I have used for the building on the right works well against the tree. If you saw this painting in tone, in a black and white reproduction, the bush in front would look only a shade darker than the orange-red building. The contrast between bush and building makes sense because of colour, not because of tone.

Red bricks against a green landscape can be difficult to paint because the colours seem to cancel each other out. One distinguished director of the National Gallery was of the opinion that more English landscape paintings were spoilt because of the colour of our bricks than for any other reason. I must agree that I feel most at home when the colour of the building blends into the landscape. But remember from p. 31 that a judicious use of red, a small dot of it, can be useful.

Many people enjoy an urban environment and it is a mistake to feel you must paint only rolling hills and dales. The townscape, buildings around you, are worth looking at. Look at the paintings of Pissarro, Seurat and Lowry; artists as diverse as these have enjoyed such places.

Detail of *Sussex Landscape*, 25.4 × 35.6cm (10 × 14in)

At Home, Looking North was painted out of an upstairs window at the back of my house. It was painted in winter and the view no longer exists; now there is a block of flats and the little bell-tower has been obliterated. I wanted to paint this at that time because I noticed that the fall of snow had changed some aspects of the view – roofs which were dark had suddenly become light. I had always wanted to paint this view, in fact I had looked at it often, but never found a satisfactory way of approaching it, chiefly, I think, because the roofs were too dark. The other point I wanted to make was that I disliked the new building in the foreground. I thought it ridiculous that at the time it was erected it had to have the wooden shed-like structures to house the water tanks, and I wanted to make it look as dull as I felt it to be. Without the little interesting vistas behind the new building I do not think I could have managed the painting.

My point here is to remind you that you can make comments, however tough, however gentle, in painting. Not all of art is about prettiness (think of Goya's horrors of war). For me, the dullness of the front of this painting makes the little details you see further back much more interesting. This is a townscape with a vengeance!

One of the most important things to notice when you are painting on the spot is the design of nature – to take advantage of what is given to you and not try to alter it. For example, the nasty light green bit on the side of the buildings in front happened to be in just the right place to balance the pink curtains in the window of the building behind. The little bell-tower happened to be in the most prominent position it could be and the fact that the roofs were lighter than the sky helped draw attention to the gentle red of the distant buildings.

On your left is a detail of two windows. The curtains were not always drawn the way you see them, but I noticed them like this on one occasion when I was painting. Do alter your painting like this, you should take advantage of a sudden change, not think of it as a nuisance.

Underneath this is a detail of the next street seen through two big walls. On the near side of the street is the snow-laden roof of a black shed. Notice how I have varied the way I have used the paint. The large walls have been painted smoothly and thinly, the shed roof smoothly and thickly, and the houses in the street rather clumsily. When I had first painted them they were carefully done rather like the walls; I wanted much greater contrast and repainted them as you see now. Take advantage of the way you can vary oil paint, you can alter the whole meaning of a passage of paint by the way you put it on your canvas. Incidentally, you can probably see how nasty the paint quality is on the near buildings in the detail opposite.

The spiky, thin shape of the little bell-tower had to be just right. Such details have to be drawn in paint very carefully; a direct contrast to the painting of the street. Beside this and below there is a dark red chimney with a light, pinkish wall above it on the right. The main mass of

At Home, Looking North, 50.8 × 76.2cm (20 × 30in)

houses in the distance is light red. I was trying to have fun
looking at all these reds together. I have bothered about
the warm colours throughout this painting. All of them
have been carefully measured together – a warm, quiet
painting which contrasts with a cool green landscape.

I have used the basic set of colours plus Crimson Alizarin,
Light Red, Raw Umber and Cobalt Blue, making ten
colours in all. This is rather more than I generally use, but
I had wanted to make the difference between the reds very
clear in this painting. This is an occasion when it is very
helpful to use a different brush for every tone of every
colour – at one time I found I had 20 in my hand. I took
three days over the painting and worked roughly from
10 a.m. until the light went. This is contrary to my usual
practice, but as I was looking north on a wintry day the
light changed very little.

*Do not add black to darken colours. Use black as a colour.
There is a difference between a black you make by mixing
several colours together and a black pigment.*

REFLECTIONS

Over the years I have been fascinated by painting water. At first I enjoyed most the contrast between the actual object and its reflection. I suppose my interest in mirrors is part and parcel of the same thing; I like the slight change of tone. The reflection is a little bit darker in tone, provided the reflection is of the same area as the object in nature – the area that you see. Always be careful if you are painting a reflection of the sky that you paint the reflection and the sky at the same time. It is very easy, particularly in our variable climate, to paint a cloudy sky and find that by the time you reach the reflection the sky is a clear, bright blue and the sky and the reflection do not agree.

Since I have been going abroad to hot climates I have found the colours in the reflections of great interest and gradually I have painted less and less of the object and concentrated more and more on the reflection, which has enabled me to keep the colours much brighter. *Collias Reflection* (opposite) is an example of this type of painting. It is a reflection of one of the spans of a large bridge.

I have found it best to do the absolute minimum of drawing because it enables me to keep the colour clear and bright. Below you can see the preliminary drawing for

Gozo Reflections, the final painting is on p. 59. This drawing was concerned only with placing things approximately. The drawing was made with a large brush, lots of turpentine and French Ultramarine. I have put a wash of colour only where the colours will be darkest. In a hot climate, a drawing will dry very rapidly, and even if you paint with more medium than usual, the paint should not pick up the underneath drawing. The drawing for *Bridge, Moor Park, Surrey* was made with thinner blue lines because the day was cold and I did not think it would dry so quickly. I prefer to do this type of painting on canvasses or boards at least 40.6 × 50.8cm (16 × 20in) large. I find I get muddled with the details if I work on a smaller size. On the other hand, I have made studies of the sea and the sky which are smaller, though I have found breaking waves difficult to paint on a small scale.

Painting reflections demands that you get your relative tones right. If you like reflections as much as I do, you will have much enjoyment painting such subjects; if you do not, I recommend you have a try so your appreciation of tone will improve.

Bridge, Moor Park, Surrey is a small painting, the sort

you might well do to see how you get on with reflections. Note how the colour of the bridge becomes much darker and cooler in the reflection whilst the sky does not. It is only a tiny bit darker in tone – I mixed up the sky and reflection together. I used normal size brushes and have not handled it any differently from the paintings we have looked at earlier.

Contrast this with *Collias Reflection*, below, which is larger and more broadly painted. The real secret when painting like this is to sit well back in your chair and paint at arm's length (or stand well back if you prefer). Always use a loaded brush, and whatever you do, do not mix up your brushes. Always paint with the tip of your brush (I know you do this by now; I only remind you because in a moment's aberration you may have forgotten) and you will find you can paint a light colour quite easily over a dark. For example, the touches of yellow have been painted over the green on the left. I had painted this bridge several times and did have the piers in several. If it gives you more confidence, put in a pier at the top.

I find it helpful to paint reflections in one sitting. The time will vary from two and a half to four and a half hours;

Bridge, Moor Park, Surrey,
24.1 × 25.4cm (9½ × 10in)

Collias Reflection,
40.6 × 50.8cm (16 × 20in)

Drawing for *Gozo Reflections*

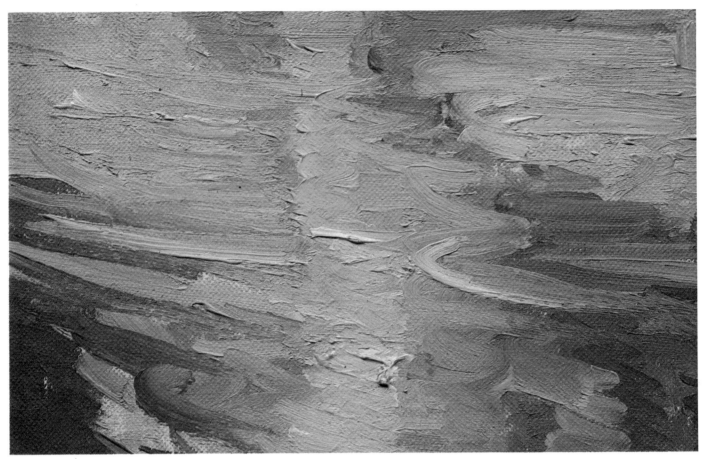

Detail of *Collias Reflection*

I find I cease to concentrate if I work longer than this without a break. Try to have enough paint on your brush so you can work in large, single strokes. Sometimes such a stroke can be a squiggle moving across quite a large area, but you *must not* go over the same stroke. Put your stroke of paint down and leave it alone. If you look at the detail from *Collias Reflection* you can see how I have put down each stroke of paint and left it alone. In the middle of the painting you will see that I have altered the first touches several times, but it is more useful to look at the left side. At the left side of the central area you can see several clear strokes of paint. All of the work has been done like this, some paint had been altered as I went along with subsequent strokes, but the fact remains that this painting has been done by putting down lots of single brush strokes.

I worked at all times with firm brush strokes. I have not filled in areas but have moved across the picture from touch to touch of paint. In the detail you can see that the little dark on the top right corner has been put down first, the light yellow strokes beside this had been put down after and the edges of the dark shape had been arrived at by drawing the lighter colour into them. Of course, the reverse was true sometimes and the dark had been drawn into the light. This is most easily seen in the final painting where the curving lines of light are drawn more firmly by the darks around them. It can also be seen in the left fore-ground, where the dark greenish colours are drawn into the blue reflection of the sky. I want to emphasize here that drawing and painting become fused, each mark is put down so it explains clearly the statement of some previous touches of paint. They are all cumulative, and the final touch brings it all together.

All this means that painting is a thinking process as well as a feeling one. I do not mean in the short term, tactical sense, but in the long term, strategic sense. You plan your picture and try to sort it out. As you go along you often change your direction, and even change your goal. Unlike the military mind, the original idea has been but dimly felt and as you proceed the aim you originally pursued is changed, not modified. There are painters whose aim does not deviate from the beginning of their sketches, but on the whole this is not the position of the beginner. You, because you are the beginner, should change your original idea often. Not because the idea was wrong, but because the most worthwhile thing you can discover is that there are many ways you could go, not at first, but when you find out what you prefer to do.

Gozo Reflections differs from the other paintings I have shown you in that it is much more brilliant in colour and at first glance appears more freely painted. I have often been asked how can I have such a free attitude to painting

Gozo Reflections, 45.7 × 61cm (18 × 24in)

when I spend so much time advocating great care with every tiny mark? I do not think that what I have done is different in concept; it is different in the way I have worked, not in the way I have thought. The motives in painting *Collias Reflection* and this picture were based upon the ideas I have talked about throughout the book. Both of these paintings depend on an understanding of tone and an ability to put the paint down in the correct place. All the drawing has been done in the act of painting.

I worked very rapidly, this painting was done in two and a half hours, with broad, sweeping brush strokes. This is one of a series I painted looking into the harbour of Gozo, a tiny island off the coast of Malta. Most of the pictures did not have boats in them, they were just about the reflections. Here, I have kept in some parts of the boats because I wanted to paint the rusty iron barrel with the wood on top and it would have been too isolated without the boats.

I started the painting at the top and quickly put in the white boat and the base of the blue boat. A few dark blue strokes took me to the edge of the barrel, where I painted the reflection of it before the barrel itself. Next came the

very dark reflection beneath the barrel and the dark 'lines' coming towards the bottom of the painting. These helped establish the flat plane of the water – the contrast between this plane and what you can see through the water is exciting. The dark lines I put down at this point have been altered to what you can see now.

The grey bluish white came next and my first concern was the straight downward part which almost bisects the painting. I was not too worried at this point about the edge of this area against the large blue area, but was more concerned with getting the correct colour. The variations in this were painted as I went along, not afterwards.

The pace at which I worked varied, sometimes I put down a large area, then drew a thin stroke across it. Try to paint like this, do not deal with all the large areas first and then go on to the details. The darker linear patterns have been painted after the lighter areas. Finally, as the light began to fade, I painted the bottom left corner.

Always have a paint rag, especially when you are painting quickly.

PAINTING WITH A KNIFE

I normally paint with brushes and my fingers, but when I work on a large scale it is nice to use a painting knife. I like the mixture of textures, playing one off against another, because you can then make the story you are trying to tell much clearer. Some people, however, prefer to paint with a palette knife all the time. As a beginner there are two times it is useful for you to paint with a knife, apart from the personal enjoyment you may get from playing about with thick wodges of paint.

If you find that you are painting in a muddy manner it is a good idea to paint with a knife – at least it will stop you going over the same stroke several times. Secondly, if you find you are painting too thinly – you are mean with a brush – turn to using a knife. At the very least, try painting with a knife and see how you get on.

There are no special subjects which are more suitable for painting with a knife; with practice and provided you do not paint on too small a scale, you can paint as many details as you like. However, for your first knife painting choose a subject like *The Silk Farm* because there are not too many details and it will give you a chance to get used to using a new tool. The whole painting was done over a period of four days. The stages represent the point at which I stopped each time.

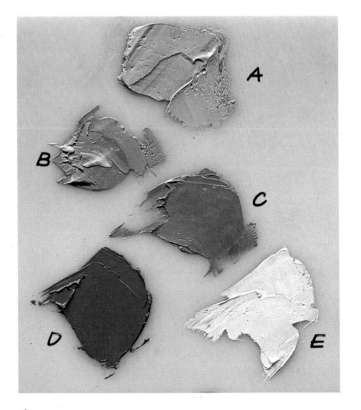

The drawing This is the only time I used a brush in this painting, there would have been no advantage in using a knife. In fact, quite the reverse is true. You want such a drawing to indicate what you are going to paint and to get in the main lines of the composition. You can see as well that I have stated the darker areas fairly simply. I do not think there is any very great advantage in doing this – it could be described as a nervous habit – except that I like drawing in tonal contrasts. Some of you might find such a habit useful because it helps keep you aware of the sense of light. I used French Ultramarine and a lot of turpentine. I used my paint rag often while planning the painting to wipe out incorrect lines.

Mixing the colours Make up quite a large quantity of paint when mixing colours with a knife. It takes me a little longer than it does when I use a brush. It is easier to use the back of the knife and you must take care to mix the colours thoroughly (traces of pure colour can be left in the mixture, with disastrous consequences when you are painting).

You can see the colours I have mixed up (left) in the first stage. Of course, these were not the only colours I had mixed up at this stage – some of the greens were necessary to make sure I had got these colours right. I used the basic range of colours plus Lemon Yellow and Cobalt Blue. I prefer a palette knife to a painting knife for mixing up colours.

First stage I started this painting at the top with the sky. I advise you to do this with your first knife painting – start at the top and work downwards – so you have no difficulty with the handling. You cannot do this throughout the entire painting, but it does stop awkward contortions at first. The sky has been put on with broad, flat strokes

A: *The sky*, White, Cobalt Blue, Cadmium Red and Yellow Ochre plus a touch of Lemon Yellow.
B: *The distant hills*, Cobalt Blue, White and Cadmium Red plus touches of Yellow Ochre and Lemon Yellow. C: *The nearer hills*, Cobalt Blue, Cadmium Red, Yellow Ochre and White. D: *The blue-accented hills*, Cobalt Blue, Cadmium Red, French Ultramarine and White plus a touch of Yellow Ochre. E: *The water tower*, White, Lemon Yellow and Red

The drawing

First stage

Second stage

across the canvas. I then put down the top part of the distant hills. Make sure that every time you pick up a new colour your knife is perfectly clean – I get through a lot of paint rag but have found large paper handkerchiefs will do as well when painting with a knife.

The water tower came next. I put it down slightly wider than it was and corrected the shape with the distant hill colours. This has been followed by the nearer hills and then the accented hills. In each case, I brought the colour down further than I wanted and placed the next colour on top of this. (You can see where the paint of the distant hills comes below the accented hills.) You can do this quite easily if you do not mess the paint about – put it down once and leave it alone. With the exception of the water tower, these colours have been put on by holding the knife horizontally and dragging it downwards. Then I added two touches of paint to the accented hills (near the water tower) with the tip of my knife held vertically. The water tower has been painted in the same manner, moving from right to left.

Second stage At this stage I began to get some of the greens onto the canvas and have started on the silk farm itself. This really had been a silk farm – the building was long so that a large piece of silk could be made and laid out. The silk worms lived on the mulberry trees, some of which still lined the roads or were dotted around the fields. The near tree in this painting is a pollarded mulberry tree.

If you compare this stage with the final painting you will see that the dark blue-greens and the colour of the near tree have been altered later. At this point I wanted to begin to establish the trees, and I found it rather easier to overstate these darks, knowing I would modify them. This does have the disadvantage of making the colour and tone in the painting unbalanced. If you find this difficult do not do it; try to make the colours correct, but err on the side of dark rather than light.

I have painted the roof of the house against the trees. I have put the dark on this in a wide stripe under the eaves, and have covered this with the lighter colour of the side of the house. The dark lines below and to the right of the house have been used to mark where I wanted the house or trees to stop and the fields to begin. Again, if you compare the light side of the house with the final version you will see that it has been painted lighter. This was done when the windows and door were added. I have also put down the beginning of the tree trunk and the beginning of the field in front of the house.

Final stage On the fourth day I began to develop the trees a little more. First I modified the near mulberry tree, making it a little lighter by painting over the very dark colours. Then I went on to the big trees in the middle-distance. I have mixed up three different colours for the grass and as I painted I have varied these colours quite a lot. The dark beside the big near tree has been altered and

Final stage

I began to repaint the house, making it a little lighter and putting in the windows and door. I have drawn in some details on the grass and put in the fence.

The fence has been painted a dark colour, onto which I have put the light. The last post on the right has been smudged and this shows the darker colour more clearly. This fence had been painted when the green was very wet. Paint details like this with the side of the knife; get a little paint all along the edge and draw it upwards or downwards, depending upon which is the easiest movement to make at that moment.

The windows and door were put down with the end of the knife in the same way as the water tower, a little too large and then corrected with the lighter, modified colour of the house. The darker edge of the far field going up to the house was painted before the fence, but the dark at the base of the fence was painted after I had finished the fence. I painted the half-tone of the trunk of the tree on the left first, then the light tone and finished with the dark touches down the side. The last areas I painted were the dark bush on the right, some darks into the trees beyond and some small touches of light green little trees into the

dark paint beside the house.

I varied the way I used the knife, but the most frequent movement was from the top to the bottom of the picture. Sometimes I found it easier to turn the picture on its side (for example, when I corrected the angled end of the house). The paint overall, except for the sky, was fairly thick. Three weeks after I had finished most of the surface was soft and great care had to be taken when stacking it against other paintings.

Painting with a knife is a much simpler process than painting with a brush, however many variations I make in any colour. Although it takes longer to mix up colours, it is considerably quicker. It is best to paint with dash and bravado, to make up your mind what you intend to do before you approach the canvas. It requires a great deal of thought first, then rapid action. It is more useful not to be too fussy about the manner in which you put the paint onto the canvas. As you paint more pictures in this manner, vary the marks you make more and more.

In general, the darker the colour you are painting, the thinner it should be; the lighter the colour, the thicker it should be.

VARNISHING YOUR PAINTINGS

You will probably have completed a number of pictures by now, some along the lines I have indicated, others launching out on your own. Remember that painting is a vast subject and there are many directions in which you can go. Remember that you are a beginner and I hope you will always remain so. The secret in art is to come to it fresh as if the subject was new to you and you had never painted before. Everyone talks of looking with an innocent eye, and what this now means for you is to learn to recapture the intensity with which you looked when you painted your first study.

Some of your paintings you will want to give to your friends, others you will want to exhibit. (Do not forget to contact your local art society, or if there is not one, form one yourself.) You will notice if you examine the work which you have been doing that it has gone 'patchy' (dull in some areas, shiny in others) and has often 'sunk' (the colour seems to have gone greyer and all the life has departed from it). Do not despair, this is the normal way that paintings dry and it can be put right by varnishing. In other words, varnish will restore the colours to their original brilliance. Just as important a reason is that a coat of varnish will protect your work from atmospheric impurities (for example, the sulphur in the air will attack certain colours if they are unprotected). Please do not be too impatient, you must wait at least nine months for your painting to dry properly. If, in the meantime, you want it to look its best for a special occasion, as a temporary measure you can apply retouching varnish. The method is the same as for a final varnish but do not wash your picture.

Preparation for varnishing

First make sure your canvas is taut by hammering the wedges at the back. Lay your board or canvas down on the table. Then 'wash' it with cotton wool. Liquid soap and water is best, but do not use a washing-up liquid because it may contain ammonia. Distilled water is ideal if you can get it. Squeeze out the cotton wool so you are not putting a lot of water onto your painting. The purpose of washing is to remove the greasy, sulphurous dirt which has accumulated on the painting – you will be surprised how much there is. Then wipe it with cotton wool dampened with clean water; ensure that you remove all traces of soap. Dry the painting with more cotton wool, and finally, with the palm of your hand, rub off any cotton wool fibres that have been caught in lumps of paint. Leave it to dry, leaning against the wall, face inwards.

Varnishing

On the next day, lay the painting flat on a table. Examine it to make sure it is quite free from any cotton wool fibres

Fig. 34

(especially at the edges). Then varnish it, being careful to brush in the varnish well. Use either Artists' Clear Picture Varnish or Picture Mastic Varnish. If it is a small picture, you can cover the whole surface with one loaded brushful. If it is a larger picture, start in one corner and finish that area (if you look at **fig. 34** you can see where I have varnished one 'square'). Then, with a loaded brush, apply the varnish in another square, starting a little way from the edge you have just done (brush the two edges together – this ensures the varnish is not too thick at the joins).

The secret of the process is to have the same amount of varnish on the brush each time, and not have too much of it. I find an old developing tray useful to put the varnish in because it has a spout for pouring the excess back into the bottle. Leave the painting flat for at least ten minutes so the varnish does not run down it. Lean it against a wall, facing inwards, to dry.

Final inspection

When the painting is quite dry (this will take one or two days, depending on the weather) examine it to see if the varnish is even, and preferably not too shiny. You can test for dryness by touching the edge of the picture to see if it is tacky. If you do not want your painting too glossy, you can use Matt Varnish (I prefer to put this over an ordinary varnish). At last, you can put it in a frame, and do not forget to admire it.